For Carmen Iona Micaela

Overleaf: *St Andrew on his Cross* by Peter Howson.
(29 November 2006)

SAINT ANDREW

MYTH, LEGEND AND REALITY

MICHAEL TRB TURNBULL

First published in 1997 by Saint Andrew Press
This revised and updated edition
published in 2014 by
Neil Wilson Publishing Ltd
www.nwp.co.uk

A catalogue record for this book is available from the British Library.
ISBN: 978-1-906000-78-3
Ebook ISBN: 978-1-906000-77-6

Printed and bound in the EU.

CONTENTS

Acknowledgements

WRITING A BOOK IS NEVER the work of one person. If the author is wise, he or she will consult a wide spectrum of authorities. In my own case this includes Jurek Pütter DA, an interpreter of the history of St Andrews, whose Grafik Orzel studio had ever an open door and Colin McAllister, whose generosity of spirit and combined enthusiasm helped to sustain me through the necessary hours of private research, the late Br John Hugh Parker, whose scholarship and insight helped me to grasp some of the finer points of Constantinian history and Professor Timothy Barnes whose advice was always incisive and thought-provoking.

I am very grateful to Creative Scotland and the Strathmartine Trust for financial research support. The many authorities who gave me the benefit of their insight are acknowledged by name in the text but I am particularly grateful for the opinions expressed by the Revd Maxwell Craig; the Revd Professor Robin Barbour; the Revd Andrew R Morton; Bishop Michael Hare Duke; the Most Revd Richard F Holloway; Archbishop Leo Cushley; the Revd John L. Bell and the late Revd Colin Morton.

Those who kindly allowed me to reproduce images include the artist Peter Howson OBE; Panteleimon Hadjiioannu; Jurek Pütter DA; AOC Archaeology; Thomas Steuart Fothringham; the late Br John Hugh Parker; The Dean and Chapter of Rochester Cathedral; Hexham Abbey Shop; Herzog August Bibliothek, Wolfenbüttel, Germany; Fife Council Museums; Robert L D Cooper, by courtesy of the Grand Lodge of Scotland; The Court of the Lord Lyon and the Order of the Thistle; Vito Arcomano, courtesy of Fototeca ENIT; St George's Society of New York; The Flag Heritage Trust; The St Andrew's Society of Philadelphia; The St Andrew's Society of Baltimore; The Victorian Scottish Union; The City of Napier Caledonian Society (NZ) and the late Revd Colin Morton. If there is any person whom I have unwittingly omitted, I ask their forgiveness and will attempt to make redress when the opportunity arises.

Foreword

A CREATIVE LEAP OF IMAGINATION is needed to locate the ties that bind St Andrew the Apostle to the Scottish nation. The theme of his story is odyssey, his method of communication networking.

The story of St Andrew grew with the story of Scotland. He has been potently utilised as a rallying point for countless Scots who left their native land in the name of a cause and who struggled to break new ground in distant lands.

The function of saints is to motivate the living by their example. From its association with St Andrew, Scotland asserts a global dimension, through links with Greece, Italy and the Ukraine. St Andrew symbolises Scotland's ruggedly individual characteristics and a unique integrity of aspiration and culture. Religious devotion, particularly in this case, is so tightly interwoven with warfare, politics, economics and sociology, as to be inseparable.

In the final analysis, religion expresses as much a human viewpoint as it does a divine perspective: it is the interaction of the two. For Scots everywhere, St Andrew has always been a focus for nationhood. He has, through the ages, been a unifying icon for preserving Scotland's identity.

Michael TRB Turnbull, August 2014

1
Andrew in the Bible

IN GREEK THE NAME ANDREW means 'manly' or 'courageous'.
Like many people of his day in Galilee, Andrew, as well as his native
Aramaic and Hebrew, would have spoken some Greek, the lingua
franca of the Roman Empire and the language in which the Gospels
were first written down.[1] This makes more credible later accounts of
Andrew's mission to preach and teach in Greece.

Although, along with the other Apostles, Andrew shared the daily
life of Jesus, what we really know about Andrew is limited to a few tan-
talising glimpses. But, in all the other events of Jesus' ministry,
Andrew can be assumed to have participated along with his fellow
Apostles.

In the Gospels, Simon Peter and his brother Andrew (who was the
younger, we are not told) first come to our notice on the shores of the
Sea of Galilee. Almost 210 metres below sea level and shaped like a
teardrop this freshwater lake is some 20 kilometres long and varies
between four and 11 kilometres in width. Its depth is around 45
metres and it has been compared to a Scottish loch, the Lake of
Mentieth being the one it most resembles.

The Sea of Galilee was
noted for fishing, boatbuild-
ing and fish curing. The
brothers Andrew and Peter,
living in the principal port of
Bethsaida (meaning 'Fisher
Home'), are ordinary fisherman, sailing craft the size of
small wooden whaling-boats
and catching the local fish
(mainly a kind of mullet).

Night-time fishing on the Sea of Galilee.
(Israeli Ministry of Tourism www.goisrael.com)

Through long experience, they would be skilled in reading the signs
of the weather, winds and currents. At the time when he was minister of St Andrew's Scots Memorial Church in Jerusalem the late Revd
Colin Morton wrote that:

In 1986, at a time when the Sea of Galilee was low and some of the seabed uncovered, a first-century AD fishing-boat was discovered buried in the mud. It was in a fair state, not complete, but sufficiently preserved so that experts could tell what it would have been like. It has been carefully preserved at Kibbutz Ginossar, kept in the dark and immersed in a wax solution for many years until the timber can withstand the atmosphere. The process has now been completed and the boat, which is called 'The Jesus Boat', is open to view. Replicas have been produced and take they pilgrims for trips on the lake so that people can experience what Jesus and his disciples did.

Fishing is still an important industry as it was in Andrew's day. Twenty-two species of fish are still found in the lake. Even today fish can gather in great numbers where hot springs well up from the bed of the lake; indeed, the shoals of fish can often be seen better from a little height on the shore than they can from the boat on the surface, bringing the story in the twenty-first chapter of John's Gospel to mind. Still today sudden squalls can spring up, especially in the afternoon and people have to watch out for them.

There have been recent archaeological discoveries at Bethsaida, which was Andrew's hometown, as it was also Peter's and Philip's (John 1:44). There had been much mystery about Bethsaida, but now very clear remains of a fishing town have been uncovered a little distance from the present shore at the flat north-east corner of the lake. People surmise that the shore in New Testament times extended further inland.

Andrew in the Gospels

In the Gospels we first see Andrew out of doors, hard at work. Matthew in his Gospel (4:18) describes Jesus walking by the Sea of Galilee when he saw two fishermen – Simon, known as 'Peter', and his brother Andrew. According to Matthew, Jesus sees the two men as they are casting nets out into the lake. And like fishermen everywhere, one of Andrew's prime personal qualities seems to have been perseverance. Next, we are told that Jesus begins to speak to them: 'Follow me and I will make you fishers of men'. Matthew records their reaction: 'they left their nets and followed him'. Whether they did so quickly, on impulse, or after mature consultation, is not clear. All we are told is who the Apostles were: 'First, Simon who is called Peter, and his brother Andrew'.

'The Calling of Andrew': bronze doors at St Andrew House, Edinburgh.

Mark (1:16) varies the account slightly. The two brothers are first seen by Jesus casting a net into the lake and that their reaction to Jesus' request to follow Him is that they leave their nets 'at once' – either a case of instantaneous conversion or spur-of-the-moment decision making. But it was still an option that they would later return to the fishing from time to time.

We next see Andrew (Mark 1:29) when Jesus is leaving the synagogue at Capernaum with James and John. All three arrive at the house of Simon and Andrew where Simon's mother-in-law is in bed with fever. The brothers immediately tell Jesus that she is ill and he goes to her and takes her by the hand. Then the fever subsides and Jesus helps her up. She starts to make them all welcome and to serve up food.

In Mark (3:18) we are shown Jesus nominating 12 men to be his companions, among them Andrew. Their primary function is to be sent out to preach, with the power to cast out devils. Much later in his ministry (in Mark 13:1-4) Jesus is seen in Jerusalem sitting on the slope of the Mount of Olives, looking at the Temple. He has just told the disciples that the Temple will one day be destroyed. In privacy, Peter, James, John and Andrew question Him: 'Tell us', they ask, 'when is this going to happen, and what sign will there be that all this is about to be fulfilled?' And Jesus tells them of the coming destruction of Jerusalem and of his second coming on the Last Day, at the end of the world. Luke (6:13) supplies the additional information that Jesus first called his disciples together and then from them chose 12 as Apostles. He adds that they were called at dawn – 'when day came'.

From John (1:40) it emerges that Andrew was influenced into following Jesus by listening to the oratory of John the Baptist, the desert preacher. John records (1:41) that it was Andrew who then first introduced his brother Peter to Jesus. John states that it was around four o'clock in the afternoon when Andrew met his brother and told him he had found the Messiah. Andrew then takes Simon to Jesus. Jesus looks hard at him and says, 'You are Simon son of John; you are to be called Cephas'.[2] John (1:44) adds that three of the Apostles – Philip, Andrew and Peter – all came from the town of Bethsaida.

Again, before the feeding of the 5,000 it is Andrew (John 6:8) who takes the initiative and tells Jesus that there is a boy in the crowd who has five loaves of barley and two fishes. But Andrew, the practical fisherman, could see no way of making these slender provisions satisfy the needs of so many people until Jesus showed him how.

Jesus and the disciples go to Jerusalem for Passover. By this time, Jesus had attracted considerable public interest through his raising of Lazarus from the dead. Jesus and his followers had been welcomed to Jerusalem with hosannas and waving palms.

John (12:22) tells us that, among those who went up to worship at the festival, there were some who were not born Jewish but had been converted. They approached Philip and asked if they could meet Jesus. Philip went to ask Andrew, and Andrew took Philip to Jesus. In John's Gospel, Andrew is presented as a personality who can be quoted and consult-

Jesus preaching to the Disciples.
E Miller, *Scripture History*
(London: T Kelly, 1838)

ed in his own right. Andrew appears to be in a position of authority. He is given a leadership role.

Our final glimpse of Andrew is in Acts (1:13). We are shown Andrew with Peter, John, James, Philip and Thomas, walking back from the Mount of Olives to Jerusalem after the crucifixion and death of their master. When they reached the city they went to the upper room where they had previously been staying.

To summarise, Andrew was, according to the New Testament accounts, a man who took initiatives. He was the first Apostle, bringing his brother Peter to Christ. He seems to have also introduced Philip to Christ. And finally, in the case of the Jewish converts in Jerusalem, Andrew was the one who took it upon himself to be the first to bring the Gentiles (those who were not Jews) to Christ. He was the first to reveal Christ to the Gentiles. This is the man our story is about.

2
Andrew in Legend

WHAT WE ARE TOLD IN the four Gospels about Andrew has a greater claim to authenticity than the strange and curious exploits which fill the pages of the later apocryphal works which claim to be truthful accounts of his life. If the New Testament gives only brief but significant glimpses of Andrew, many versions of the probably second-century *Acts of Andrew* – and Acts of other Apostles – imaginatively elaborate the story of his teaching and preaching and locate his mission-field as in Greece and Asia Minor.

Over the centuries the subsequent 'labours' of Andrew were piously worked up into a fantastically heroic tale, full of exaggerated miracles and of horrendous torment, sermons said to have been given by the saint and the supposed evidence of miracles he had worked. These accounts are plainly attempts to turn Andrew into a folk-hero embodying many of the spiritual characteristics of the countries and cultures for which the stories were written and reminiscent of the epic and fantastical exploits of the Greek hero Heracles, known in Latin as Hercules. These descriptions of Andrew's superhuman achievements were meant to be pious vehicles of Christian teaching but their exaggerations later consigned them to the category of apocryphal material of doubtful authenticity.

Agios Andreas (St Andrew's Church), Patras.
(Courtesy of Panteleimon Hadjiioannu)

Only the very bare bones of Andrew's life and character are known and this made it relatively easy for pious stories to be invented to fill the biographical gaps. The slender biographical details of Andrew's life were a fertile seedbed for the preacher or the travelling storytellers in the market-place or around the fire, to embroider as they thought fit. These later traditions record that Andrew preached in Greece, in the Ukraine, Poland and also in the early settlement of Byzantium (which would later become Constantinople and finally the modern Istanbul).

Andrew is believed to have been imprisoned and tortured in the city of Patras in Greece and then left to die on a cross by the seashore close to where the church of Agios Andreas (1908) stands today. Traditionally the date of his death is celebrated as 30 November, the day of the month Andrew shares with the death of the Greek play-wright Euripides (406 BC) and the birth of the Anglo-Irish satirist Jonathan Swift (1667). Today historians regard many of these tradi-tions as being at best impossible to verify and at worst as pure specu-lation. But even if these widespread and spectacular traditions are largely pious fancy aimed at attracting the popular imagination, nev-ertheless the extraordinary miracles and exploits of Andrew were to play an important part in the religious culture of the Middle Ages.

Andrew is also mentioned, for example, in the apocryphal *Gospel of Peter* (written around AD 150) and later in the *Epistle of the Apostles* (around AD 160) where Jesus invites Andrew to look at his feet and see if they made prints in the ground, since the ghost of a devil was said to leave no footprints on the ground.

The Alexandrian scholar and teacher Origen (AD 185-254) writes that Andrew also had a mission in Scythia (southern Russia). But even as early as the fourth century, there were those such as Bishop Philastrius of Brescia in northern Italy who complained that the fables about Andrew and other Apostles, in which they were made to work miracles where dogs and cattle were given human voices and souls, were clearly exaggerated and even heretical. Later writers gener-ally accepted the fact that Andrew was martyred in Greece around the year AD 70 but were sceptical as to the genuineness of his and the many other saints' mummified bodies and relics.

The many versions of the *Acts of Andrew* existing before the year AD 200 developed four distinct but related cycles of stories – Egyptian, Byzantine, Latin and Syriac. According to these texts the exploits of Andrew were colourful and awe-inspiring. First we are told that the Apostles drew lots as to where they were to preach the message of Christ. Andrew is said to have been told by Jesus in a vision that he must find a boat and sail to Sinope, the City of the Cannibals on the Turkish coast of the Black Sea. As they set sail, Andrew and his companions sudden-ly find Jesus sitting at the rudder, piloting the ship. Some authorities believe this Black Sea mission took place about the year AD 44.

St Andrew with St Philip.
E Miller, *Scripture History*
(London: T Kelly, 1838)

Andrew is said to have driven out devils in Nicea in northern Turkey and it is claimed he also travelled to Thrace in the southern Balkans and Sevastopol in Crimea. It is said that in Sinope he found the inhabitants preparing to eat several human captives. Andrew prayed to God but the Devil appeared and encouraged the people to turn against Andrew. They tied a rope around Andrew's neck and dragged him through the streets, tearing off pieces of his body so that his blood flowed like water on the ground. But Andrew somehow managed to escape and afterwards fruit trees grew on the spot where his blood had been spilled. Next Andrew continued his journey through Thessaly in northern Greece until he came to Patras, the capital of Achaia on the Peloponnese. There his conversion of the local people enraged the Roman proconsul Aegeates, particularly when Andrew persuaded the proconsul's wife, Maximilla to reject the pagan gods.

Andrew was imprisoned by Aegeates who had him scourged and crucified in Patras on the sands at the seashore. Andrew's hands and feet were not nailed, but tied to the cross. From the cross, Andrew preached to the great crowds standing around him until he died. Maximilla took Andrew's body down from the cross, washed and embalmed it and buried it on the seashore beside the prison. From that time Maximilla lived apart from her husband. Aegeates, however, was driven insane by guilt and the separation from his wife and eventually threw himself to his death from the roof of his official residence.

Such is the main storyline, which varies in detail from one version to another. The long rambling sermons of Andrew, and the sadistic descriptions of his torments, are evidence of history running out of control, of fact at the service of propaganda, however well intentioned. The lurid and exaggerated details of the apocryphal *Acts of Andrew* are very different from the low-key, commonsense narrative of the Gospels.

Other writers allege more personal biographical details about Andrew. He is, for example, said to have been unmarried – unlike Peter, who had a wife and children. He was older than Peter but was baptised by him.

There is no mention of what we know today as the 'Saint Andrew's Cross'. Andrew is said to have been crucified upright (unlike his brother Peter, who was crucified upside-down). Andrew is said to have been tied (not nailed) to a forked or Y-shaped olive-tree. However, this shape of cross was, around the tenth century, developed into an X-shaped (*decussate*) one – which mimics the Greek letters *Chi Rho* (XP from the word 'Christos'). The crossed keys of the Roman papacy would also reflect the *Chi Rho*, but with this difference: each key also embodied the structure of the *fasces* – the bundles of

St Andrew on the cross. (Jurek Putter).

rods and axes carried by the *lictors* (attendants or magistrates) in Imperial Rome to symbolise the authority of the law.

As to the geographical scope of Andrew's apostolic activity, the most reliable source is the first Church historian, Eusebius of Caesarea (AD 260-340) who states that Scythia was assigned to the Apostle Andrew. After Andrew's death, the city of Sinope, which he is said to have visited, proudly claimed to have a pulpit (*ambo*) from which Andrew had once preached. The stories of Andrew's visit to Russia and the conversion of the quasi-mythical ruler Bravlin are also to be found in one of the first entries in *The Tale of Bygone Years* (the *Primary Chronicle*). The *Chronicle* is thought to have been compiled between AD 1100-1200 by two monks from Kiev, Nestor and Sylvestor, who drew upon older annals and legends which have not survived. In the *Chronicle* it is written that Andrew, after teaching and preaching in Sinope, set off for Rome travelling via Cherson in the Crimea, the Dnieper river, the land of the Slovenians and even to Scandinavia.

His first stop (the *Chronicle* tells us) was at what would eventually become the city of Kiev. There he raised a wooden cross on the surrounding hills, blessing the land and promising that one day it would become Christian. He predicted the construction of a great town full of churches. When Andrew journeyed on to Slovenian territory, he arrived at the site of the future city of Novgorod on the Volkhov

River. As an observant traveller, Andrew is said to have been intrigued by the Slovenian custom of sauna baths. These were taken in heated wooden huts, followed by whippings with thin branches of trees and finally cold water showers. Many of these legendary accounts of Andrew's missionary activities probably originated in Egypt and Syria and from there were introduced into Byzantine Church circles. Their main source was probably a report of Andrew's apostolic activity that can ultimately be traced to the *Apocrypha* generally regarded as of heretical, often Gnostic in origin and which, from the fourth century onwards, were frequently mentioned and specifically rejected by the early Church Fathers. They were composed in the second or at the beginning of the third century, probably in Greek in Achaia or by an Egyptian.

Gnostics (from the Greek *gnosis* – knowledge) believed that they, and they alone, had a special revelation from God which would ensure their salvation. For the Gnostics, the physical parts of God's Creation were evil. In their view, Christ was God but not human; he had been sent to rescue particles of spirit (*souls*) trapped in matter. Hence, the *Acts of Andrew* promote an over-exaggerated emphasis on a rejection of the values and cultures that Andrew encountered in his mission.

A short version of the original *Acts of Andrew* is preserved in a Greek manuscript now at the Vatican Library, Rome. But the intriguing *Acts of Andrew* survived, at least in part, in some other western and eastern adaptations – including Ethiopian and Coptic texts written in Christian communities of Africa.

3
Constantine the Great

ONE OF THE PRACTICAL APPLICATIONS of St Andrew was that he was a very malleable saint, whose biography was porous enough to allow him to be used for motivating communities to achieve a broad spectrum of goals. It is said, for example, that during one particular European military campaign three different armies fought each other, each under the flag of St Andrew. In the early Church the lives of saints were important as mission statements in the struggle for salvation. St Andrew had an indisputable apostolic pedigree and a genealogical route through Peter to Christ. This offered the Church not only doctrinal authenticity and continuity of priestly ordination, but also, when necessary, political and even military credibility.

Andrew's was a proactive life of initiative and conspicuous virtue, not mere passive holiness. In addition, Andrew was believed to have travelled widely, he was transnational. But, unlike Paul of Tarsus, Andrew left no personal correspondence or developed moral teaching. In the course of time, he developed into an effective symbol for nationhood, rather than a cardboard historical figure – a multi-purpose embodiment of Christian strength of character.

Following his apostolate as recorded in the Gospels, the most significant event in the development of Andrew the saint took place on AD 28 October 312 on the outskirts of Rome. The central role of the cult of Andrew in Scottish history cannot be fully understood without reference to the crucial battle for superiority fought between the rival emperors Constantine I and Maxentius on the northern approach to Rome at the Milvian Bridge over the River Tiber.

Constantine was no stranger to the Roman province of Britannia. He had proven physical links with the territory that later became the England and Scotland that we know today. Although early English historians would later suggest that Constantine was born in Colchester and that his grandfather was King Coel (the 'Old King Cole' of nursery rhyme), he was in all probability born at Naissus in Serbia on 27 or 28 February around the year AD 272.

His Turkish-born mother Helena (who would later gain fame for her discovery of the Cross of Christ outside Jerusalem in AD 326) accompanied his father, the Emperor Constantius I (who may have already been a Christian and was certainly sympathetic to Christianity) to Britannia in AD 305. Constantine, by that time already a military tribune, fought alongside his father on his last campaign into the north of Scotland to subdue the Highland tribes early in AD 306.[3] Constantius claimed a victory against the Picts and was awarded the title of 'Britannicus Maximus'. He retired to York for the rest of the winter but then, in the middle of summer on AD 25 July 306 he died there with Constantine at his side. As he lay close to breathing his last, Constantius recommended Constantine as his successor.[4]

Bronze statue of Constantine outside York Minster.
(Author's copyright)

On Constantius' death the legions at York hailed Constantine as Augustus, the embodiment of the sun god, and they placed the imperial purple on his shoulders. This most probably took place at the legionary fortress in what was then Eboracum, the headquarters (*principia*) of the northern imperial command, on a site that can still be seen today under the nave of York Minster. Many centuries later, when archaeologists came to investigate Traprain Law in East Lothian, two coins of the Emperor Constantine the Great were found on the slopes of the Hill.[5]

Within six years, however, Constantine faced the most critical event in his long life. Standing between Constantine and the undisputed control of the Western Empire was his fellow emperor, Maxentius, whose enemies had branded him a tyrant. Constantine was

Coins of Constantine and Maxentius.
(Author's collection)

determined to become supreme Emperor of the Roman Empire in the West. Accordingly he marched his army from Gaul across the Alps into Italy and set his sights on Rome. In his search for religious legitimisation he had already put his trust, first in the god Hercules, then changed his devotion to the worship of the god Apollo and Sol Invictus, the Unconquered Sun. Constantine was sympathetic to Christian beliefs but had not been baptised. Interestingly evidence has recently been found of the worship of the sun god at the Roman fort in Inveresk, just east of Edinburgh, as early as the second century AD.[6]

Writing a quarter of a century after the Battle of Milvian Bridge, Eusebius, Bishop of Caesarea (AD 275-339) and the biographer of Constantine, explained that the emperor believed that to defeat Maxentius he needed not only military power but divine intervention. Maxentius had enlisted the help of black magicians and psychic powers. He was reported to have consulted the Sibylline oracle's prophecies before the battle, the supposedly divinely inspired words of the Sibyl of Cumae, near Naples – at that time preserved inside the Temple of Jupiter on the Capitoline Hill in Rome where they were always consulted in national emergencies.

The prophecy Maxentius received from the auguries was: 'On this day, the enemy of Rome will die'. Maxentius, a senior emperor, had persecuted the Christians and was as

Second-century Altar of Sol Invictus, excavated at Inveresk. (Courtesy of AOC Archaeology)

superstitious as Constantine but, unlike the latter, said to be debauched and depraved.

Constantine had held back from converting to Christianity, even though there are clear indications that his mother, and perhaps also his father were Christians. Indeed it was not until he was on the point of death in AD 337 that Constantine was baptised. Since baptism wiped out all previous sins, it was the custom at the time to postpone baptism until the last moment of life. In AD 312, although sympathetic towards Christianity, he was not convinced that it was right for him. But, he was a pragmatist, willing to try anything if it achieved success. He decided to test if Christianity could secure victory on the battlefield. If he won, he would give his allegiance to Christ; if he lost, he would take it as a sign that the Christian God was not supreme.

The Vision of Constantine, Chapel of St Anthony the Eremite, Murthly, Perthshire.
(Courtesy of Thomas Steuart Fothringham)

According to Bishop Eusebius, God heard Constantine's prayer for victory and sent him a sign in the sky. In the rays of the setting sun, the emperor and his army saw the Greek letters *Chi Rho* (XP) clearly outlined in the sky in the blazing refraction of the rays of the sun as it sank down the horizon. At first he did not understand what this dazzling sunset meant. Constantine only grasped its deeper meaning when he had fallen asleep.

He dreamt that Christ urged him to use the sign he had seen in the sky the next day when he went into battle. When Constantine awoke early in the morning of 28 October, he called for the Christian priests who were already in the camp. They explained that the *Chi Rho* was the symbol of Christ's victory over death. Constantine understood that he would conquer only if he adopted the *Chi Rho* as his insignia[7] and immediately gave orders to fly the *Chi Rho* on a cavalry standard at the head of his army. He ordered the symbol to be painted on the shields of his soldiers and had a golden *Chi Rho* soldered onto his own helmet.

Meanwhile as the moment of battle approached, Maxentius made the most of his position. Central to his defence was the Milvian Bridge, built by the censor Marcus Aemilius Scaurus

The Milvian Bridge, Rome.
(Courtesy of Br John Hugh Parker)

in 109 BC over the River Tiber at the northern approaches to Rome. The bridge already had some political significance, as it was there that Cicero captured the messengers of the Gallic tribe, the Allobroges, in 63 BC at the time of the Catiline conspiracy. Between the bridge and the city, two miles to the south, Maxentius had constructed a complex system of forts and trenches to supplement the protection of the city walls. Close to the bridge he had built a sturdy pontoon of boats lashed together to provide additional access for his forces. He was secure in the overwhelming superiority of his army and had also taken good care that the old gods and the oracles were on his side.

The battle began and raged fiercely. However, slowly and against all odds, Maxentius' men were forced back to the Milvian Bridge. Soon it became too narrow for the soldiers trying to withdraw across it. They made for the alternative route – the new floating bridge. Then, at the height of the fighting, the ropes holding the pontoon of boats together gave way unexpectedly under the enormous pressure of retreating men. Hundreds of soldiers from the defending army were thrown into the water, Maxentius among them.

In his historical record of the battle Eusebius compares the confusion of this moment to the scene in the Bible where Pharaoh and his Egyptian army are swallowed up by the waters of the Red Sea – 'they sank like a stone' (*Exodus* 15: 5). Seeing this, the jubilant song of triumph from Constantine's victorious army rose to the skies.

Maxentius' body was found, where it had been thrown up at the side of the river. His lifeless head was cut off, impaled on the point of a lance and given pride of place in Constantine's triumphal entry procession into Rome. Allegiance to Christ had little effect on the ruthlessness of the victor, schooled in the discipline of the Roman army. Constantine needed to demonstrate unequivocally to the Roman people the finality of his victory and the dawning of a new era.[8]

Inscription at the Milvian Bridge. (Courtesy of Br John Hugh Parker)

For Constantine, the Battle of Milvian Bridge was a moment of personal conversion. The defeat of Maxentius placed Constantine at the head of the western half of the Roman Empire. As the late Br John Hugh Parker has observed, 'Constantine added Christianity to the list of officially-approved religions of the empire'.[9] He paved the way for Theodosius the Great 'who made Christianity the religion of the empire ... about 390 AD'.[10]

The Battle of Milvian Bridge would, in later centuries, hold a special significance for the whole Christian Church, as it marked the beginning of the defeat of the old gods and their mysteries and the ascendancy of the new Christian religion of light. The sun had become identified with the Son. In later days Constantine would display the *Labarum* – as the new Christian standard was called. It was made from a long spear wrapped in gold with a crossbar forming the cross. On the spearhead a golden ceremonial wreath studded with gems was fixed. In the middle of the wreath was the *Chi Rho*. From the crossbar there flew a cloth woven from golden thread, richly embroidered, while between the wreath and the banner were portraits of Constantine and his family, formed from sheets of beaten gold.

* * *

As the years passed one of Constantine's priorities was to rebuild Rome as a fitting capital where heaven could touch earth. Among his many projects was the basilica built over the shrine of St Peter, only to be completed in AD 349 after Constantine's death. On 8 November AD 324, Constantine renamed Byzantium, the ancient eastern centre of Christianity by the Bosphorus. He called it 'Constantinople'. There, on the site of what would later become the Church of the Holy Apostles, he erected a circular mausoleum for his own burial.

Print of Constantinople. (Author's collection)

After Constantine's death in AD 337, his body was interred in the mausoleum. Twenty years later, Constantine's son, the emperor Constantius II, built a cruciform basilica next to it where he deposited the relics of the Apostles Timothy (AD 356) and Luke and Andrew (AD 357), the latter taken from Patras. These had been forcibly collected by the armed agents of

Constantius and would have almost certainly involved considerable outrage among the communities who saw their objects of traditional piety and income from visiting pilgrims brutally removed.

Eusebius described the Church of the Holy Apostles in Constantinople as being built very tall in elevation, with porticoes on its four sides and on its walls, with marble cladding right up to the gold of the domed roof. At the heart of the church were 12 empty caskets designed to receive the remains of the Twelve Apostles.

However, in spite of Constantius' orders, it would appear that, in the case of Patras at least, some parts of the body of Andrew were quickly and secretly removed by the local clergy – notably (as later events would suggest) the head. Whether this implies that an alternative skull was substituted, is not clear. It is possible that the mummified body, wrapped in linen and perhaps in a wooden coffin, may have been removed by Constantius's agents, without checking that all its constituent parts were present or that they were the original body and not a substitute.

Writing many centuries later, in the 1440s, Walter Bower, the Augustinian abbot of the monastery at Inchcolm Island in the Forth estuary, imagines the legendary St Regulus (Rule) spiriting away some parts of the St Andrew's body – three fingers of the right hand, a humerus, one tooth and a kneecap. Although it seems likely that some of the body parts may have been secretly substituted in Patras, the older Latin and the much later Scottish accounts differ as to which parts of the skeleton were concerned.

In Patras the body of the saint might already have been washed and de-articulated into its 206 component bones. It would have received the attentions of the most sophisticated reliquary technicians of the day, skilled in the art of making as many relics as possible, so as to support the faith of believers all over the world. The body of Andrew had been venerated at Patras where it had been buried, it is said, by Maximilla after being taken down from the cross on the shore. Constantius' policy of collecting the bodies of Christian heroes was aimed at increasing the status of the churches in his new capital. It also served to underline the integration of the secular with the religious power. In AD 397 what were claimed to be the relics of the pre-Christian prophet Samuel were also transferred to Constantinople.

Constantine's body was later moved by his son Constantinus from the original mausoleum in Constantinople to the new, golden-roofed, Church of the Holy Apostles nearby. St John Chrysostom (Bishop of Constantinople AD 398-404) states that the emperors were buried in the outer vestibule, beside the other relics of the saints. During the Fourth Crusade (1202-04) the church was destroyed and remained a ruin until the Fatih Mosque was built on the site (1463-1470). However, some idea of its magnificence can be gathered from the design of the Basilica of St Mark in Venice. It is understood that St Mark's with its onion domes was inspired by the architecture of the Church of the Holy Apostles.

The onion domes of St Mark's, Venice. (Vito Arcomano, courtesy of Fototeca ENIT)

Relics

It was imperial policy, based on the original wishes of Constantine the Great to be buried in Constantinople, that the city should become an international repository for the relics of the saints. Accordingly they were systematically and deliberately brought together to Constantinople from all over the known world. By 1200 they are thought to have numbered around 3,600 relics from 476 different saints.[11] Relics were the mortal remains of holy persons, or objects sanctified by contact with them. The first relics venerated by Christians were those of the martyrs who were tortured and put to death until the persecution of Christians was revoked following a meeting in January AD 313 in Milan between Constantine and Licinius, the Emperor of the East. Issued jointly, one of the results of the meeting was the Edict of Milan.

Primary relics (parts of the bodies of saints) were venerated as signs of the victory of Christ's sacrificial death repeated in the death of his saints. *Secondary* relics (cloth which had been placed over the bodies of the saints accompanied by the most solemn prayers and known as *brandea*), were at first frowned upon, but eventually became accepted as instruments through which God could work. From the fourth century onwards, bodies of those considered to be saints were exhumed, dismembered and distributed to local churches, especially to Alexandria, Antioch and Constantinople. Constantinople, a newcomer with few native martyrs' remains from the pre-Constantinian persecutions, worked hard at gathering relics.

Among the vast collection of relics brought to Constantinople were the Instruments of the Passion, two pieces of the True Cross, the Pillar at which Jesus was scourged, the Crown of Thorns, the Sponge and the Sacred Lance used to pierce Christ's side.

The cult of relics developed from an established belief in the power of 'virtue' (from the Latin *virtus*). In the Gospels virtus is used on only a few occasions. It refers to the healing influence of Jesus, such as was shown in the case of the woman who had suffered from an issue of blood for 12 years (*Luke* 8: 43-50) or the preaching of Jesus to those who had come to him to be healed from disease. (*Luke* 6: 17-19)

Andrew would have been present at the healing miracles which Jesus performed in touching a sick person: 'When the local people recognised him, they spread the news through the whole neighbourhood and took all that were sick to him, begging him just to let them touch the fringe of his cloak. And all those who touched it were completely cured.' (*Matthew* 14: 34)

Jesus cures the Blind Man.
(E Miller, *Scripture History*,
London: T. Kelly, 1838)

Specific cures of this nature include the healing of the deaf man (*Mark* 8: 31); the blind man at Bethsaida, Andrew's own town (*Mark* 8: 22); the man suffering from leprosy (*Luke* 5: 12); the woman with a haemorrhage (*Luke* 8: 40); the crippled woman (Luke 12: 10); the son of the widow of Nain. (*Luke* 7: 11)

The healing power of the words of Jesus nevertheless required an act of belief and self-surrender on the part of those who wished to be healed. It was not magic, but an interaction. In the early Church the display and veneration of relics became a powerful method for building a sense of commitment and motivation in the believer.

One would hesitate to say that an 'industry' in the presentation of relics gradually arose, but it was a highly specialised task which required all the skills of the undertaker, the anatomist and the priest and authenticity would be confirmed through wax seals and certificates.

The original tombs of the saints would be reverently unearthed and opened, often many years after their death, when only the bare skeleton would be left in the grave. The bones of the saints would normally be washed into a disarticulated skeleton of more than 200 separate bones. Then they would be wrapped and placed in a new container which would form the core of a shrine. This process of enshrinement was known as *translatio* (translation or *commutatio*). These visible burial places of the martyrs had a key function in the development of the early Church and the translation (or deposition) of relics was often celebrated annually as a special feast day.

In Italy the principal initiator of the cult of the Apostles was St Ambrose who built a church in Milan dedicated to them. In it he placed relics of Andrew, John and Thomas that he had obtained from Constantinople. Every May the deposition of these relics was solemnly commemorated.

Even at this early period, other Italian cities claimed to have relics of Andrew. Paulinus, Bishop of Nola – who was born in AD 353 near Bordeaux, became Bishop of Nola c.AD 409 and died AD 431 – is found congratulating himself for having obtained relics of Andrew and Luke for his basilicas in Nola and Fondi. The city of Concordia in Lombardy also possessed some relics of the Apostles, including those of Andrew.

The theologian Bishop Gaudentius of Brescia, who died around AD 410, writes that in his day Andrew was greatly venerated in the Western Church. He boasts that his church in Brescia contains relics of John the Baptist, Andrew, Thomas and Luke. He apparently also obtained relics from St Ambrose.

In Ravenna in the Emilia-Romagna region of Italy, there were fifth-century monuments dedicated to Andrew. Theodoric the Great, King of the Ostrogoths, ruler of Italy (AD 493-526), built a church (destroyed in 1457) in the name of Andrew and dedicated it to the cult of the Goths. The Goths seem to have had a particular veneration for Andrew. His feast is commemorated on 29 November in a fifth-century Gothic calendar composed in Thrace in the south-eastern Balkans. Petrus Chrysologus of Ravenna, who died in AD 450, commemorated Andrew's feast day with a sermon in which he confirmed that the saint was crucified on a tree.

In Ravenna Bishop Peter II (AD 494-519) built a chapel to St Andrew, in his own palace, while Bishop Maximian (died AD 546) restored the church of St Andrew and placed more relics there brought over from Constantinople. In Constantinople itself, during the demolition of the old basilica soon after AD 548, relics of Andrew, Luke and Timothy were rediscovered and placed in a new building constructed by the Emperor Justinian.

Maximian had wanted to take the body of St Andrew to Ravenna but the emperor was determined that the New Rome (Constantinople) must continue to possess the relics of St Peter's brother. However, by a trick, Maximian succeeded in obtaining what was said to be the beard of St Andrew, which he then took away to Ravenna.

The cult of St Andrew grew in Rome particularly during the Acacian Schism (AD 485-519). There, the feast of St Andrew was celebrated in the fourth century, preceded by a vigil and fasting. The first Roman basilica dedicated to Andrew was erected on the Esquiline Hill by Pope Simplicius (AD 468-83). Pope Gelasius I (AD 492-6) also built an oratory in honour of Andrew on the Via Labicana. Near the basilica of St Peter, Pope Symachus (AD 498-514) constructed a rotunda dedicated to Andrew.

In France, St Victricius, Bishop of Rouen (who died at start of the fifth century) mentions the deposition of relics of Thomas, Andrew and Luke in his cathedral. According to the historian Gregory of Tours (c.AD 538-94), there were relics of St Andrew preserved at Neuvy not far from Tours.

During the fifth century, copies of the fanciful stories of the *Acts of Andrew* circulated in the West. Pope Innocent I (AD 402-17) mentions them, while Turibius, a contemporary of Pope Leo the Great (c.AD 390-461), warned the faithful against reading them.

For later centuries, much of the popularity of Andrew is due to the historian Gregory of Tours who edited a book about the achievements of Andrew. Leaving aside the many stories that he considered to be exaggerated and therefore heretical, he chose some of the miracles of Andrew and the adventures he experienced along the shores of the Black Sea. Andrew had become a folk hero in the mould of Sinbad the Sailor.

Gregory of Tours, among many colourful stories about Andrew the Apostle, also recounted the unlikely miracle which cured a certain Mammolus who, in the sixth century decided to visit Andrew's tomb to be cured of prostate problems – mainly his inability to pass water. The saint, according to Gregory, answered Mammolus' prayers and he eventually passed a colossal stone!

There had been, up to this period, however, no attempt to connect Andrew with the beginnings of Christianity in Byzantium through the person of Stachys, whom St Andrew was supposed to have instituted as Bishop of Byzantium. Nor is there any evidence that Andrew was being used (as he would later be) as a figurehead to increase the status of Constantinople to rival that of Rome.

In AD 573, the future Pope Gregory the Great was Urban Prefect (head of the senate) when his father, one of the richest men in Rome, died. Within the next 12 months, Gregory transformed his family home on the Coelian Hill into a monastery dedicated to St Andrew, with a style of living based on the Rule of St Benedict (c.AD 480-547).

St Benedict of Nursia, Patron Saint of Europe. (Author's collection)

Today, with its oratory of St Andrew, the building is known as San Gregorio Magno. Gregory went on to found six monasteries in all. Half-a-century later, in AD 625, Pope Honorius I, perhaps inspired by Gregory's example, also turned his Roman home near the Lateran into a monastery, dedicated, like Gregory's, to St Andrew.

Meanwhile, Rome, poorly defended, became an easy prey to the Lombard invaders. Desperate for reinforcements, Pope Pelagius II sent Gregory to Constantinople as papal legate to the new emperor, Mauricius, whose acquaintance Gregory had made while Mauricius was still a serving soldier with a distinguished military career. From AD 579 to AD 586, Gregory served in Constantinople. In his *Dialogues*, he confesses that in order not be too much immersed in secular matters when at Constantinople, he brought with him some monks from his own monastery of St Andrew. Perhaps his desire to remain detached from the exotic social life of Constantinople also explains why Gregory quite unashamedly admitted that, during all his time in the city, he had not learnt to speak a word of Greek.

However, he could not fail to notice the great number of relics now collected in the city. Shortly before he left for Rome, Gregory persuaded the emperor to give him a number of them for his monastery. Chief among these was the head of St Luke and the arm of St Andrew – 'arm' probably signifying the hand, the lower and upper arm-bones and the shoulder blade.

When Gregory reported back to Rome, Pope Pelagius II promoted him to be his secretary of state. Only a year later, Gregory set off on a mission to England but was recalled. In AD 590, Gregory, still only a deacon, was, by the command of the emperor, made Bishop of Rome, assuming the reins of office even before he had been ordained a priest.

4
St Andrew in England

FROM THE DEATH OF POPE Pelagius II in February AD 590, the Papacy was vacant for almost seven months prior to the election of Gregory as pope on 3 September. Then disaster struck Rome. The Church's wheat granaries were swept away by floods and torrential rain. To make matters worse, the city fell into the grip of plague. Gregory, confirmed in his new office, gave orders for a penitential procession through the city with sung invocations to God and the saints. This took place on three days in succession, the faithful desperately chanting *Kyrie Eléison* ('God have mercy' in Greek). As they marched, people in the procession could be seen collapsing and dying in the streets.

Kyrie Eléison – Society of St John the Evangelist, Plainsong for Schools. (Liverpool: Rushworth & Dreaper Ltd., 1953), p 4

The hostile weather and the scourge of disease which tormented Rome served only to challenge Gregory. He saw himself as captain of the ship of state and the barque of Peter, struggling to hold his course and reach dry land. Gregory wrote to his friend, Leander, Bishop of Seville:

> Although battered by the wind and rain, I do not let go of the rudder ... I turn to face the storm. When the ship lurches to one side I steer through the heaving sea. The stinking cargo of sin which we carry makes me cry out in anguish. Over the howling gale, I can hear the frightening crack of the ship's timbers breaking. Wiping back my tears I glimpse the tranquil land of my dreams which I will never see again. As the anger of the hurricane forces me away, I snatch a sight of the shore and groan.

Central to Gregory's understanding of the Church was the belief that it was not only Holy and Catholic, but Apostolic – founded by the and connected to the Apostles by an uninterrupted Episcopal succession. Key, in this respect, was the conviction that the Church's dogmas were based on the teaching of the Apostles which, in turn, derived directly from Christ.

'Not angles but angels' – this famous play on words is said to have been delivered by Gregory five years later when, in the autumn of AD 595, he came upon slaves from Britain standing in the marketplace. Gregory was so struck by the noble savagery of their appearance that he ordered the 17 and 18 year old youths to be purchased by the Church and placed in monasteries at Rome to be trained for the service of God. His intention was that one day they would be sent back to their homeland as missionaries.[12]

Gregory had been approached by Christians among the Angles who asked him to send out missionaries, as the local bishops made no effort to preach the Gospel to them. Gregory invited 40 of the monks from his monastery of St Andrew to go as missionaries to Britain led by Augustine, a Benedictine monk. They left Rome in the spring of AD 596 and reached Provence in France. Morale among the monks was low, so Augustine returned to Rome and was given a letter by Gregory. 'Do not let the difficulty of the journey nor the evil tongues of men alarm you', he wrote and enclosed letters of introduction to the bishops on their route to Britain and they were duly told to retrace their steps.

When they reached France, the missionaries were joined by a number of local priests who were to act as interpreters in England. The historian Venerable Bede (AD 672-735), a Benedictine monk at the Northumbrian monasteries of St Peter, Monkwearmouth and St Paul's in what is modern Jarrow, tells us that just before Easter AD 597, Augustine landed on the Isle of Thanet in Kent (probably at Ebbsfleet). Gregory's correspondence hints clearly that Augustine landed only when he had been certain of King Ethelbert's welcome. King Ethelbert insisted on hearing him preach in the open air. The king's wife, Bertha, was a Christian and had helped to ensure that her husband would welcome the missionaries. That Christmas, more than 10,000 Angles were baptised. Moreover, as Augustine had informed Pope Gregory that he had a great harvest, but few labourers, Gregory sent along an increased supply of fellow workers and ministers of the Word.

The most influential personalities among these recruits were Mellitus, Justus, Paulinus and Rufianus. With them Gregory also sent all kinds of materials which would be needed for the service of the church – sacred vessels, altar draperies, church ornaments, vestments for bishops and clergy, relics of some of the holy Apostles and martyrs and a supply of books. Gregory continued to write letters to encourage Augustine's missionary team and inform them of a far-sighted policy decision. Augustine was told to incorporate into their Christian rituals those elements of pagan practice which were acceptable to Christianity. At the same time, he was anxious to make use of what religious buildings already existed, once they had been suitably cleansed. 'Do not pull down any of the pagan shrines', he wrote. 'Destroy only the actual images of the pagan gods which they contain. Then bless holy water and sprinkle it over the shrines. Finally, make altars and place relics inside them'.

At Canterbury, Augustine and his monastic community dedicated their first monastery to Saints Peter and Paul, the patron saints of Rome. Later, in AD 604, King Ethelbert erected for them a church dedicated to the Apostle Andrew. Further north, St Andrew's Priory in Rochester, a Saxon cathedral later to be destroyed at the Norman Conquest, was probably not a stone building. Yet, even in the present (third) cathedral, St Andrew's Day is still annually celebrated.

12th-century Norman cloister at Rochester Cathedral. (Robbie Munn: Courtesy of the Dean and Chapter)

The crypt of Saints Peter and Paul was modelled on that of St Peter's, Rome, which, with that of St Paul, was the shrine to which pilgrimages from the northern nations came most frequently.

Often the long-term success of evangelisation rested on a knife edge. Making converts was one thing, but keeping them quite another. One of the major problems facing Augustine and his fellow missionaries was consolidating the faith of those who had been newly baptised. Much depended on the protection and encouragement of local kings. When Ethelbert died in AD 616 and was buried in St Augustine's Abbey at Canterbury, power was transferred from Kent to Redwald, King of the East Angles.

A backlash against Christianisation now threatened the work of Augustine, particularly when there were kings such as Eadbald, who had never been baptised and who revolted from Christianity. And, shortly afterwards, Seberht, King of the East Saxons, died leaving three sons who soon reverted to the old pagan religion. Then Bishop Justus of Rochester abandoned his see and retired to Canterbury where he remained for 12 months.

However, reciprocal contact between Britain and Rome grew steadily. As early as AD 726 King Ine of Wessex (the territory of the West Saxons), who died in Rome in the same year, founded the church of San Spirito in Sassia (which survived until it was rebuilt in 1540) specifically for Saxon pilgrims.

In AD 627 a timber church was erected over a spring in the city of York and there on Easter Sunday, King Edwin was baptised. Edwin appointed York, the principal town of Deira, as the see of Paulinus and began to build a basilican church of stone around the wooden oratory.

At Ripon, St Wilfrid's church was said to have been built on the site of an ancient British church but it also had a crypt. Hexham, also one of Wilfrid's churches, had a similar crypt. One of key figures in the development of devotion to St Andrew, Wilfrid was born in AD 634 and entered the monastery at Lindisfarne in his teenage years. In AD 653, with Benedict Biscop, he left for Rome, travelling with him via Lyon. There he was introduced to Pope Eugenius who placed his hand on Wilfrid's head, prayed over him, and blessed him. In Rome, Wilfrid went round the shrines of the saints with his companions, making a collection of relics, each carefully labelled

Entrance to the Crypt, Hexham. Abbey. (Author's collection)

with the saint's name. He also bought purple cloth and silk vestments to decorate his churches. Then, with the blessing of the saints upon him, Wilfrid set off in the peace of Christ, armed with the holy relics he had collected, and so returned safely to England in AD 658. After the Synod of Whitby (AD 664) he was elected bishop of Northumbria and consecrated according to the Gallican rite at Compiègne in northern France.

By AD 678, Wilfrid had gained control over extensive territories. King Ecgfrith, alarmed at Wilfrid's growing status, demanded that the diocese be split into four. Wilfrid appealed over Egfrith's head to Rome – the first recorded appeal to Rome by an English prelate.

Again Wilfrid travelled to Rome, where he won his appeal. On his return to England, however, he was imprisoned and exiled by Ecgfrith, who had defeated a Pictish revolt around AD 672 and seems to have secured recognition of his authority even from the Scots of Dal Riata and the Britons of Strathclyde. However, in AD 685 he was killed in battle at Nechtanesmere at Dunnichen and from that time the hopes and strength of the Northumbrians began to ebb away.

After Ecgfrith's death Wilfrid returned to Hexham, regaining the see of York and the monastery at Ripon. Once again, in AD 691, Wilfrid quarreled (this time with Aldfrith) about land and went to Rome again to fight his case. Of Wilfrid's church at Hexham, dedicated to St Andrew and constructed (originally of wood) on royal land, no certain trace remains above ground. Only the famous stone crypt survives. Hexham became a cathedral in AD 678 and was subsequently enlarged by Bishop Acca. Wilfrid's is probably the most famous early crypt still in existence in the northern half of Western Europe. The church at Hexham had been dedicated to St Andrew by Wilfrid in AD 674 and the relics of the Apostle Andrew were brought there later by Acca – either on one of his many visits to Rome or from the relics originally brought over from Gregory's monastery in Rome and placed in St Andrew's, Rochester.

As Christianity crept northward into Northumberland, more churches were built in honour of St Andrew by the missionaries from Rome. The two Apostles who were to be most steadily and continuously honoured in England were St Andrew and St James. St Andrew is one of six or seven saints common to all the 40 counties of England where there were to be between 600 and 700 pre-Reformation churches dedicated to him. Of these, 570 were ancient, (including the cathedrals of Wells and Rochester). It is also worth noting that in pre-Reformation England there were only 106 churches dedicated to St George.

Wilfrid had proceeded with the erection of churches in the northern portion of his see which extended to the River Forth. Indeed, he regarded the Picts as being under his special charge. When Wilfrid fell into disfavour, he was imprisoned for a time in Dunbar in East Lothian. In Rome in AD 680, Wilfrid spoke publicly on behalf of the Picts, declaring them to be faithful children of the Church. Accordingly, in the following year, a separate bishop of the Picts was appointed, who took Abercorn in Linlithgowshire as his seat.

After the battle of Nechtansmere the church of North Britain was finally separated from that of the south.

As for Wilfrid, he died at Ripon in AD 709.

5
The Relics Go North

ALTHOUGH THE PURPOSE OF AUGUSTINE'S mission to Kent was to introduce Christianity through persuasion and example, Pope Gregory (perhaps remembering the very real military threat which had led in AD 579 to his own posting to Constantinople) did not hesitate from advocating, when expedient, the use of warfare as a means of forcible conversion. The pagan rulers of England were sympathetic to the concept of a 'holy war' because belief in the God of the Christians evidently held out the proven promise of a better-than-even chance of victory in battle. In this, they were not much different from the Emperor Constantine when he became convinced that he needed to embrace the insignia of Christianity at the battle at Milvian Bridge. It was certainly a pragmatic and self-seeking reason for fighting under the flag of Christ but, apparently, immensely efficient in that it achieved the desired result.

In seventh- and eighth-century Britain Christian spirituality could motivate effectively. Augustine's mission preached a revitalised vision of Christ brought directly from the monastic community of a new and dynamic pope. The old pagan beliefs had often become tired from long familiarity and were failing to grip the imagination of their adherents.

As Christianity moved north from Kent, making converts, it gained momentum from the activities of bishops such as Acca of Hexham (c.AD 660-742), St Wilfrid's chaplain in the last years of his life, and his close companion. On Wilfrid's death in AD 709, Acca succeeded him as bishop and enlarged and enriched his church of St Andrew, collecting yet more relics of the saints from his frequent journeys to Rome, building up his library, teaching liturgical music and using his wide experience as a theologian to explain and promote the Christian faith.

The Venerable Bede held Bishop Acca in great regard, dedicating a number of books to him, some of which Acca had also commissioned. But, in spite of all his gifts and achievements, Acca was suddenly and inexplicably expelled from his episcopal see, never to return. It is possible that he had been caught up in the dynastic conflict following attempts to depose King Ceolwulf – a local ruler who would himself later abdicate and become a monk at Lindisfarne. Acca had been a staunch supporter of Ceolwulf and may even have been a relative. When the latter was forced out of office in AD 731, Acca was one of the immediate casualties.

According to Simeon of Durham, Acca was driven from his see in AD 731 or 732. Rumour had it at the time that he had gone to found a bishop's see among the Picts. There is also a suggestion that Acca may even have stayed for some time in the south-west of Scotland at Whithorn in Galloway.

Only a few years after Acca's forced departure from Hexham, the bishopric of St Andrews was founded by a Pictish king called Óengus (Angus). It is not certain which Pictish king this was – either Angus I, son of Fergus (AD 729-61) or Angus II (AD 820-34). In both cases, they were Pictish warlords and over-kings of the kingdom of Fortriu (southern Perthshire). While no direct link can be proved between the two events, a connection between them seems highly probable.

Acca's exile and consequent search for royal patronage provided a strong motivation and an opportunity, along with the availability of the Apostle's relics. A royal monastic foundation at Kilrymont (later St Andrews) is historical fact and the location of Andrew's relics at Kilrymont was certainly accepted common belief. The cult of Andrew the Apostle had, after all, followed the corporeal and non-corporeal relics of the saint. His bones had moved steadily northwards from Patras to Constantinople, then (in two separate operations) to Rome and, later, to Amalfi. Finally, relics were taken to Canterbury, Rochester, Hexham and to Scotland.

Royal patronage was the key to stability. The primary function of new religious foundations was often to strengthen the power of kings. Political circumstances immediately north and south of the Firth of Forth were becoming receptive to such foundations. Supreme kings were emerging to weld smaller monarchies together. Economies of scale were in evidence as territories and possessions were forcibly merged through aggressive military expeditions. This general process was taking place in the eighth and ninth centuries as ethnic groupings were forced together by Pictish supreme kings. This was accompanied by the development of the cult of new saints and the creation of genealogies of the kings to justify their right of inheritance.

In the Early Church, a 'saint' had first been a member of the baptised Church or the faithful departed. Gradually the term was also extended to cover martyrs. In the case of Scotland in the eighth century, the saint whose heroic missionary endeavours still resonated most strongly was Columba (AD 521-97), the Irish Apostle of Christianity, raised in the royal warrior aristocracy of Donegal. Columba's monastery on the island of Iona became the mother church of Celtic Christianity in Scotland. Other saints, such as Ninian (fl.AD 390), the earliest ordained Christian leader in Scotland, were widely venerated.

In the eighth century the church of the Picts had first identified itself with St Peter as its chief patronal saint, perhaps in the reign of King Nechtan (c.AD 600-30), and finally with St Andrew, possibly during the reign of Angus I. Both kings ruled over a long and reasonably stable period. During the reigns of Nechtan and Angus and also that of Constantine, King of Picts (AD 789-820), attempts were increasingly made to model the role of the king on that of the Roman Emperor, Constantine the Great. In fact, there were three kings of Alba named after the emperor – Constantine I (AD 862-79), Constantine II (AD 900-c.943) and Constantine III (AD 995-7).[13]

In Western Europe, after around the year AD 750, especially during the life of the Holy Roman Emperor Charlemagne (AD 747-814), the Constantinian model of kingship grew in importance. Charlemagne, known as 'The Father of Europe', had subdued and Christianised the kingdoms around him, especially those of the Saxons and Lombards. The exploits of his chief *paladin* (warrior), Roland, had produced the heroic literature of the *Chanson de Roland*. In AD 800, Charlemagne marched his armies to Rome in support of Pope Leo III, who in gratitude crowned him Emperor of the Romans in St Peter's Basilica. But warfare was no more than a necessary evil. Charlemagne's administration was also characterised by effective and just laws, by stability and peace, all ensured by military supremacy. Charlemagne encouraged the growth of education, agriculture, industry and commerce. For the Pictish kings – and, later, the Scots – this made his achievement and that of Constantine the Great well worth imitating.

The legends surrounding St Andrew

Out of the many differing manuscript accounts that surround the development of the cult of St Andrew, there is a core narrative sequence with which all the surviving historical records broadly agree.

It begins with the assertion that somewhere south of the Firth of Forth, a Pictish king was motivated by belief in St Andrew to conquer

in battle. As a consequence, a Pictish king encouraged and supported the establishment of a shrine to Andrew the Apostle at what was
to become St Andrews in Fife. However, from the standpoint of the
21st century, it is not at all clear whether the two stories were or were
not connected or that the two Pictish kings were one and the same
person.

There are two slightly different narratives of the battle and the
foundation of the shrine. Both of them attempt to explain the significance of what happened by citing the foundation legend as resulting
from the outcome of the battle. Both narratives, however, have more
elements in common than they have differences.

The first narrative was probably compiled at St Andrews in the
Royal Hall, perhaps by a Culdee (Celtic *céli dé* – 'companions of
God') monk. It seems to be a sermon for St Andrew's Day, and may
have been based on previous homilies written not later than the early
12th century.

The second narrative is thought to have been composed for King
Ferath, son of Bargoit, who reigned c.AD 840. However, it is more
likely to have been written in the 11th or 12th century. The two versions share a basic storyline but differ in details.

Unfortunately, no contemporary eyewitness descriptions survive
either of the battle or of the foundation of the shrine. The two narratives are both based on early written and oral records of the battle
and of the foundation that have been lost or destroyed. The first surviving record is found in a late 12th-century manuscript that was once
part of the library of the Cistercian abbey at Newminster in
Northumberland. Another surviving manuscript was written at York
around the year 1360. An alternative account dates from the 14th
century. It was surreptitiously removed from St Andrews for a
Continental antiquarian at the time of the Scottish Reformation and
today is in the Herzog August Bibliothek at Wolfenbüttel, Germany.[14]
Another similar narrative survives only as an 18th-century transcript
of a now-lost manuscript originally written at St Andrews.

The common thread of the story which is contained in both narratives is that the relics of Andrew were forcibly removed from Patras
to Constantinople and a Pictish king was victorious in battle through
the intervention of St Andrew. Bones of the saint were taken by a
monk from their resting place in the Eastern Mediterranean. Then,
the bones were carried to Cennrigmonaid (in Scots, Kilrymont, later
St Andrews). Finally, the monk and a local king co-operate to found
a church dedicated to Andrew the Apostle.

In the first narrative, we are presented with a king called Angus I, son of Fergus. Prior to doing battle, he observes a blinding flash of light and hears the voice of St Andrew. He is victorious with the saint's help.

The second narrative concerns the Pictish King Angus. At the same time that St Rule reaches Muckross in Fife, the Apostle Andrew is recorded as appearing to Angus, promising victory over his enemies. This narrative was used by John of Fordun in his *Chronica gentis scotorum* (1384-7).[15] Fordun (died c.1384) is thought to have been a chantry priest in Aberdeen. His work is the chief authority for the history of Scotland prior to the 15th century. Fordun completed the history down to 1153, but left collections extending to 1383 which were added to and completed by Walter Bower (c.1385-1449), an Augustinian canon, born at Haddington in East Lothian.[16]

While folk mythology may have speculated about the origins of the Scots, the Venerable Bede's opinion had been that the Scottish nation had come from Scythia in southern Russia, one of the territories said to have been evangelised by St Andrew. Walter Bower, on the other hand, proposed that the Scots were descended from the Greek prince Gaytheolos and his Egyptian wife Scota, daughter of the Pharoah Chencres who had died in the Red Sea while pursuing the Israelites. This may partly explain the biblical echoes which are frequently to be found in the descriptions of the Pictish King Angus and the Greek St Rule (also known as *Regulus*).

There seems to have been on the one hand, some residual folk memory that races and peoples had migrated over the centuries from the Middle East to the north of Europe. However, historians also took care to establish the authenticity of kinship between mythological or biblical figures and the people of the contemporary world. They were trying to show connections between the half-remembered past and the intrusive present – trying to provide evidence of the brotherhood of man and the continuity of Creation.

The two narratives of the Battle of Athelstaneford differ. The first states that Angus was conducting a military campaign in the northeast of England with mindless destruction and the utmost barbarity – the implication is that he is not at this point a Christian. He decides to rest up with his troops in the Merse but is soon surrounded by a force drawn from all the nations in Britain, who have but one aim in mind: to put him and his whole army to death.

In the second narrative (and Walter Bower's account in the *Scotichronicon*) St Andrew appears to King Angus in a dream. Angus is walking with his seven closest advisers when they are bathed in a supernatural luminosity. They fall flat on their faces onto the ground and hear a voice from the sky saying: 'Angus, Angus, listen to me, Andrew, an Apostle of Christ. I am sent by God to defend and guard you. Just look for the sign of the Cross of Christ in the air where it advances against the opposing army. Make a donation of a tenth of your possessions both as a sign of gratitude to Almighty God and in honour of St Andrew'. According to this narrative, Angus divides his troops into 12 units. In front of each unit was carried a standard displaying the Cross of Christ, from the tip of which shone an unearthly light. Clearly an echo of Constantine at the Milvian Bridge but also grounds for legitimising the religious foundation at St Andrews.

The Battle of Athelstaneford

Athelstaneford, like Milvian Bridge, was a watershed in Scottish history, the symbol of a decisive turning point where Christianity finally succeeded in winning over the most influential royal, civic and military backing.

While there is little doubt that a series of skirmishes or a battle such as Athelstaneford took place at some date and at some place, we are, with the foundation of the church at Kilrymont, on much surer ground, since it refers to an easily recognisable institution – the site of what eventually became the great cathedral church of St Andrews. The geographical location of the battle, however, is in some respects relatively insignificant. There are no major towns or buildings associated with the battle, only a hamlet and a small stream.

The location for the battle specified in this first narrative is Mercia (central England south of the Humber between Wales and East Anglia), rather than the interpretation current in Scotland as being the Merse (the low-lying land between Lammermuirs and the River Tweed).

If Athelstaneford was indeed the location of Angus' crucial battle, then it may have had some strategic significance as being on a route from England to what would become Edinburgh. The modern village of Athelstaneford is 262m/794ft above sea level. It lies two miles north of the River Tyne and borders a plain surrounded by fortified hilltops. Three kilometres (1.9 miles) to the north-west, beyond Kilduff Hill, is the Iron Age hill fort at Chesters, defended by an elaborate system of ramparts and ditches. At a similar distance to the west are the Garleton Hills (highest point Skid Hill at 610m/2001ft), with another hill fort looking east. About six kilometres (3.7 miles) to the south-east is the important hill fort of Traprain Law, which flourished during both the Iron Age and the Roman occupation between AD 78 and AD 215. To the east is Markle, said to be a corruption of 'miracle' and supposed to mark the place where the Cross of Christ was seen shining in the sky.

To the west in the valley just below Athelstaneford, the Cogtail Burn rises in the Garleton Hills, running under the Cogtail Bridge until it flows into the Firth of Forth. Beside the burn a long Christian burial cist was once discovered. Just above the bank of the burn is the Hanging Craig and not far south again, the remains of another hill fort.

Traprain Law from the west. (Author's copyright)

The earliest record of the Battle of Athelstaneford does not describe the colour of the sky and refers to the vision of King Angus as the Cross of Christ shining above him. In later centuries the cross was said to be that of St Andrew, which imitated the *Chi Rho* symbol of the Emperor Constantine I at the Milvian Bridge in AD 312 outside Rome.

The entry in Bishop William Elphinstone's *Aberdeen Breviary* (c.1431-1514) for the feast of St Regulus records that Angus was baptised after the battle at Kilrymont by St Regulus. Taken with previous suggestions that Angus waged war with extreme and unnecessary cruelty, we are justified in concluding that Angus, like Constantine (but for different reasons), was not a Christian at the time of the Battle of Athelstaneford. Constantine, after all, was not baptised until 16 years after the Battle of Milvian Bridge – when he was at death's door.

There are several contradictions in the accounts of the battle. John of Fordun identifies the hostile leader as Athelstan who outlived Angus II by several years. However, there may be confusion here with the enemy of Scots – the King of Wessex. In the second version, the enemy is a king of the Saxons called Adelstan (who is beheaded after his defeat by the Picts).

The summit of Traprain Law. (Author's copyright)

Some historians place the battle during the reign of Angus I and identify the opposing king as Eadbert whose general was Athelstan. Alternatively, the hostile king may have been the Athelstan who ruled nearly all England south of the Humber and who, in AD 934, planned to conquer the lands to the north. He managed to penetrate as far as Dunfoether (Traprain Law). As for the location of the battle, Fordun translates this from the Latin as Tynemouth in Northumbria, while Walter Bower in his *Scotichronicon* places the site at Athelstaneford in East Lothian.

The placename 'Athelstaneford' may come from the Pictish *Aith-ail* [stone-ford] – 'stepping-stones'. This might have been added later to the Anglian equivalent 'staneford' to give 'Athelstaneford'. The spot where the defeated Athelstan was pulled off his horse and killed was next to the Cogtail Burn, previously called the Rugdown or Lugdown from the Scots 'rug' (to pull). The vision of the Cross of Christ was reputed to have been to the east, over Markle Farm – the name of the farm assumed to be a corruption of the word 'miracle'.

It is worth remembering that Bower himself was born in Haddington and would have undoubtedly visited the site of the battle on several occasions as a boy and perhaps later also, when preparing the text of the *Scotichronicon*. While explaining that there were three English kings called Athelstan, Walter Bower includes a long quotation from the English chronicler, William of Malmesbury (c.1090-1143) to support his assertion.

Bower goes on to say that the death of Athelstan at the hands of Angus is fresh in his readers' memory, both from a variety of historic documents and from an oral tradition still alive in his day. It is this oral tradition, in particular, that Bower can have been expected to have absorbed most vividly during his childhood and schooling in Haddington.

Of course, that is not to say that everything that Bower writes about the Battle of Athelstaneford is necessarily totally accurate. What it does underline is that Bower's sources were not confined to manuscripts alone, but included his own experience of a living oral tradition in East Lothian and, probably, interviews he may have conducted as part of the information-gathering process for the *Scotichronicon*.

Bower writes that Angus, at the height of a campaign against the Anglian monarchy (in which he and his army had caused immense devastation in Northumbria), decided to set up camp two miles from Haddington on a fertile plain half-a-mile above what is now Athelstaneford. His intention was to give his army time to replenish supplies and to rest after their exertions. The location he had chosen had abundant fields of corn and grass, woodland shrubs, springs and rivers. It was also on an eminence (which would give him plenty of warning of an attack) and was well sheltered, with abundant lookout points at the hill forts to the north and to the west. From the description we can assume that the time of the year was late summer.

Athelstan, meanwhile, assembled a large force and caught Angus off guard, surrounding the much smaller army of the Picts. Fear and deep pessimism gripped Angus and his generals. They understood too well that there was no way of escape. The only thing they could do was pray.

Speaking in his capacity as a senior cleric, Bower adds that God never fails to help those who sincerely ask for divine assistance. Accordingly, Angus and representatives of all the ranks of his army made vows to God and the saints, especially Andrew the Apostle.

The text of the *Aberdeen Breviary* for 9 May (the *Translation* of the bones of St Andrew) indicates that Angus had enemies within his own Pictish ranks. He is said to have executed some of his lords and to have faced a conspiracy by others. We can also conclude that some devotion to Andrew may have been already established among the Picts.

The following night, while Angus is asleep, St Andrew appears to him. He tells him that he himself has pleaded the cause of the Picts with Almighty God who, says St Andrew, always answers the request of those who pray with sincerity and humility. Angus can be confident of victory the next day,

Sunrise over the Garleton Hills near Athelstaneford.
(Author's copyright)

because he and many of his soldiers would see an angel holding the Cross of Christ at the head of his army as they broke free from the encircling Anglian force. But Angus will only conquer if he gives God a tenth of his wealth immediately after the battle.

Bower adds that St Andrew reminds Angus that his vow was made without any physical or psychological pressure, but with the fully conscious use of his free will. The indisputable meaning of this theological footnote is that Angus would not on any legal grounds later be justified in dismissing his promise as having been made under duress and therefore not being binding.

If he were to renege on this solemn vow, he would be guilty of grave sin. Perhaps we are to understand that in St Andrew's mind – and in that of Walter Bower as he addresses the temporal leaders of his day – there must have been the strong likelihood that Angus would be tempted not to fulfil his part of the bargain. However, like the Emperor Constantine before him, Angus enters into a transaction with God, whose reward is physical survival but whose price is a tenth of his worldly goods.

When Angus wakes again, he describes everything in his dream to his generals and soldiers. Immediately their morale rises dramatically. They are changed men, fired up with unprecedented courage and aggression. The Picts attack, although outnumbered, screaming and blaring trumpets to startle and disorientate their enemies.

The Anglians are terrified. They break ranks and desperately begin to retreat. Only the king and his immediate bodyguard stand firm. But in a short time even they are surrounded and put to the sword. Athelstan's head is severed from his body and, by order of Angus, placed in a prominent position on the island of Inchgarvie, visible to everyone crossing over the River Forth from what is now Queensferry.[17] Bower's account of the display of Athelstan's severed head stuck on a wooden pole (a mere four miles south-west of Bower's own scriptorium at Inchcolm and one of the established pilgrim routes to St Andrews) is suspiciously anachronistic.

If the admittedly questionable interpretation by the historian and Reformer George Buchanan of 'Markle' as 'miracle' is correct as indicating the location of the vision of the Cross of Christ seen by the Picts, then it was seen to the east of the battle site. This would suggest that what the Picts saw in the sky was the early morning sun refracted against a summer sky – rather than the distinctive cross of clouds suggested by the Scottish author Nigel Tranter in his novel *Kenneth* (1990).

In heraldic terms, the white saltire cross (widely flown in Scotland and used in the badges of societies or businesses) is a representation of silver. The early morning sun, glittering silver, fits this interpretation as to how the Scottish saltire was first perceived. As it was for Constantine at Milvian Bridge, the *Chi Rho* became a mesmerising guarantee of victory as Angus and his men began their offensive. The death of Athelstan is effected at the crossing-point over water. Like Maximian, Athelstan has his head severed and publicly displayed as a sign of triumph and as a warning.

But the overarching meaning of the battle is the victory of the institutional Church and its close association with military and economic power. 'God is the ruler of all kings', Andrew tells Angus in his dream. The story of the appearance of St Andrew to Angus in a dream is repeated by most of the later Scottish historians – John Major (1469-1549); Hector Boece (c.1470-1536); the reformer and Renaissance scholar George Buchanan (1506-82); John Spottiswood (1565-1639) and John Leslie (1526-96). Bower's version of the story is deftly compressed by Buchanan in his *History of Scotland*, a 20-volume work completed shortly before his death.

Two centuries later the parish minister, the Revd George Goldie, writing in the *First Statistical Account of Scotland* (1791-99) and acknowledging his indebtedness to Buchanan's *Rerum Scoticarum Historia, adds that ' ...* towards the end of the twelfth century, the parish churches of Athelstaneford and Crail in Fife, with their tithes, were annexed to the monastery of St Martin, in the parish of Haddington, by Malcolm IV.'

The *Second Statistical Account of Scotland* (1845), however, appears to contradict Goldie:

> History records that the lands on which the battle of
> Athelstaneford was fought and won, were given by the
> King of the Scots to the Culdee Priory of S. Andrew, as
> an acknowledgement of gratitude to Heaven for the vic-
> tory obtained. At the Reformation, when monkish insti-
> tutions were abolished in Scotland, these lands were
> conferred on the Chapel Royal of Holyroodhouse, with
> which they are still connected, and form a considerable
> part of the income drawn by the present dean or deans
> of that venerable fane. The late Sir David Kinloch,
> Baronet of Gilmerton, obtained from the Crown a per-
> petual lease of these lands.

Taken together, these two pieces of information appear to confirm that the battle site passed into the ownership of the ecclesiastical authorities at St Andrews and they offer a convincing reason for the land being so assigned. In addition, we learn that the land was of considerable monetary value – presumably for farming.

The viewpoint at the Scottish Flag Heritage Centre,
Athelstaneford, over the fields to North Berwick Law.
(Author's copyright)

Interestingly, the *Ordnance Survey Name Book* (1853) contains the military surveyors' handwritten report of their mapping activities at Athelstaneford. One of their informants – a local farmer, told how he had been quarrying for stone some years previously, and had unearthed a Christian long cist burial just to the south-east of the Cogtail Burn bridge.

The *Second Statistical Account* fills out the story:

> In the cist was found the badly-decayed remains of a warrior, including part of the human cranium and the lower jaw. The coffin was but two and a half feet below the surface. It was formed of five handsome freestones –

one at each side of the body, one at the head, another at the feet, placed at right angles, and one for covering. The stones forming the coffin had been cemented together with a fine paste made apparently of clay, to prevent the admission of the external air. A cavity had been cut in the surface of the hard rock, six feet two inches in length, thirty inches in breadth, and four in depth, in which the body had been laid, and where it was found.

This was believed to have been the body of the unfortunate Athelstan, who had been in headlong flight when he was killed by an arrow. However, if Walter Bower is correct in saying that the head of the vanquished leader was displayed on an island in the Firth of Forth, then the skull in the Athelstaneford cist is unlikely to be Athelstan's.

The Ordnance Survey places the site of the battle on a wide, flat piece of ground to the north of Athelstaneford and to the west of the B1347, just south of the now-disused East Fortune airfield.[18] At one time there were two standing stones: one at the southern limit of the battle site (near Athelmead), the other (near Greenburn) at the northern edge. One stone has since been destroyed, the other removed.

While the Roman Emperor Constantine's decision to accept the patronage of Christ made it possible for Church and State to be identified in a united Christocentric empire, Angus' acceptance of Christ through his Apostle Andrew also led, through the relics of Andrew, to the foundation of a national shrine in a kingdom united and centred on Christ.

The *First Statistical Account of Scotland*, enthused by George Buchanan's stately narrative, boasts proudly that 'it was Achaius, King of the Scots ... by whose assistance Hungus [Angus] obtained this victory, [for he] afterwards instituted an order of knighthood in honour of St Andrew'. In memory of the occasion, Kenneth II (AD 971-95), King of Scots, is believed to have instituted a royal Order of St Andrew.

Around the reign of Kenneth II, a version of the *Acts of Andrew* was transcribed into Old English. The 1,700-line Andreas was found in northern Italy in the archives of the Cathedral of Vercelli. The city of Vercelli is on the main pilgrimage route to Rome and also has a 13th-century church dedicated to St Andrew.

In the poem, the Twelve Apostles are presented as warriors, in the style of a Viking epic – 'glorious heroes'. Andrew is celebrated as a heroic missionary, sailing through violent storms (like the Greek St Regulus), who by his sufferings persuades others to receive the bath of baptism, abandon idolatry and destroy the old pagan altars. With the help of angels and through the power of God, Andrew receives supernatural help. He becomes invisible for a time in order to defeat his enemies. Although he is tortured near to death, his blood fertilises the earth, turning it, where it falls, into gardens of lush trees and fragrant flowers.

Andrew becomes not only a bringer of the Good News but symbolises the fruitful nature of conversion and the tangible harvest which, according to the poet, will follow any nation's acceptance of the power of the crucified Christ.

6
The Voyage of Rule

ACCORDING TO WALTER BOWER'S *SCOTICHRONICON*, a Greek monk, St Regulus (anglicised to Rule), keeper of the Apostle Andrew's relics at Patras, is warned by an unnamed angel to remove some of the saint's bones from his sarcophagus at the shrine, hide them and then wait for further instructions. Two days later, the legions of the emperor Constantius captured the city of Patras, stripped it of all its wealth and forcibly transferred the Apostle's relics to Constantinople. The removal of the relics is said to have been on AD 3 March 357.

The pillaging of Patras and the removal of its relics shocked the community of believers. Perhaps the dramatic story of St Regulus and his voyage arose from a desire to minimise religious unrest. It covers over the sensitivities of communities who wished to move on. The 'Voyage of Rule' pulls together some threads of history, recalling the Samson in the *Book of Judges* who discovered that the rotting carcass of the lion he had killed was now inhabited by bees producing honey – 'out of the strong comes forth sweetness'.[19]

The story of the voyage from Patras to St Andrews clearly is a later re-working of historical events aimed at explaining the arrival of the relics of St Andrew in Scotland compressing complex historical processes and events by means of an accessible and memorable 'parable'. The name 'Regulus' (meaning the Rule of Obedience under which religious congregations lived) is very probably a symbolic figure for the Augustinian Canons Regular at St Andrews and their rule of living. The Augustinians had periodically edited and updated the St Andrews foundation legend and were responsible for displaying and guarding the Apostle's relics in St Andrew's Cathedral for the religious education of believers and the conversion of non-believers.

The first version of the legend tells us that, following the battle of Athelstaneford, the victors were in a quandary as to where to make the religious foundation that God required of them. In answer to their prayers, their fasting and appeals to the mercy of God, a monk named Regulus, one of the guardians of the body of the Apostle

Andrew at Patras, had a visionary experience in which God revealed to him that, protected by a guardian angel, he must leave his own country, his way of life and his home and go to the land that God would show him – Mount Royal, known as Kilrymont in Fife.

Walter Bower, in a second narrative describes God's directive to Regulus quite differently. He writes that after a passage of several years, the same angel again appeared to St Rule and, with a fearsome expression on his face, told him to take the relics he had previously hidden and sail westwards to the ends of the Earth. Rule obeyed and after many adventures, he and the monks and nuns sailing with him, left the Mediterranean and headed north past the coasts of Portugal and France, through what is now the English Channel and up the east coast of Britain.

The journey ended when Rule and his fellow passengers were almost killed in a shipwreck. According to the angel, this was a sign that Rule should walk ashore and end his journey. There, on the headland, above the rocks, Rule is ordered by the angel to build the foundations for a church. The angel also told Rule that, just as people flocked to the East to hear Andrew preaching, in future times, pilgrims would come in great numbers to pray at his new shrine in the West and be cured by the miraculous healing of the relics of the Apostle.

This second narrative of the story specifies the relics Rule has secreted as being three fingers of the right hand, an arm-bone from between the elbow and the shoulder, one right kneecap, a single tooth and part of the skull. This information is also contained in The Letter-Book of James Haldenstone, prior of St Andrews (1418-43).[20]

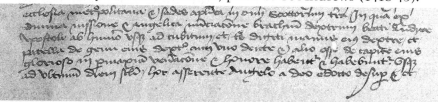

Description of the Relics of St Andrew held at St Andrews Cathedral, from the *Copiale Prioratus Sanctiandree*, No 65 in Codex Helmstedt 411. (With the kind permission of the Herzog August Bibliothek, Wolfenbüttel, Germany. See Chapter endnote 20.)

The arm, it is assumed, was part of the collection of relics brought back from Constantinople by Pope Gregory, placed in his own monastery in Rome and partly transferred to England either by Augustine, Wilfrid or Acca. They became the source of the relics that formed the centrepiece of devotion in the cathedral of St Andrews.

From the year AD 787 it was a requirement re-emphasised by the Seventh General Council of Nicea, that every consecrated church should have a relic placed in its altar. However, a clear distinction was made between devotion paid to the Virgin Mary and the saints, and the worship reserved for God.

Latria (total worship) was due to God alone. Saints were to be venerated (*dulia*) and the Virgin Mary was accorded an enhanced veneration as Mother of Christ (*hyperdulia*). In practice these distinctions were not always understood by the people, so giving rise to abuses of exaggerated attention to the importance and power of the saints. Saints were not to be venerated for themselves, but only in so far as their lives gave evidence of *grace*, the love and saving generosity of God. As outstanding examples of His Creation, they were believed to offer Christians an additional means of accessing the love of God. Meditation on the lives of the saints was also a way of focusing prayer. Time and again, the Latin of medieval manuscripts repeats the phrase '*Deo et Sancto Andreæ*' ('To God and Saint Andrew'), emphasising that St Andrew is subordinate to Almighty God, to whom alone worship is to be given. The relics of Andrew are to be accorded veneration but never *worship*.

The second version of the legend in addition distinguishes between the varieties of places of worship which Rule and King Angus set up. These are: *oratories* (small chapels); *ecclesias* (equivalent to a parish church) and *basilicas* (major churches or cathedrals).

The foundation legends for the shrine of the Apostle Andrew at Kilrymont do not correspond in terms of the forensic accuracy which we would expect of historical records today. Nevertheless, running under the different versions of the legend, it is possible to pick out a number of strands of information which are likely to have a factual basis.

There are two discrete but interlinked stories in the legend – the Battle of Athelstaneford and the arrival of St Rule. Both take place in the east of Scotland. The first occurs inland and south of the Firth of Forth; the second, on the coast and to the north of the Firth. This helps to impress the universal applicability of the legend to all Scots. It is worth noting that there are other legends of the time which link the Lothians with Fife. The mother of the apostle of the Celtic kingdom of Cumbria, St Kentigern (or Mungo, c.AD 518-603) was said to have been the daughter of Loth, King of the Lothians. At his fort on Traprain Law (only a few miles from Athelstaneford), Mungo's mother, Princess Thenew was hurled off the steep southern side of

Traprain Law for becoming pregnant by a shepherd. She survived and managed to cross the Firth of Forth in a coracle to Culross in west Fife where her son, Mungo was born.

Walter Bower emphasises for his readers that St Andrew will be a sure foundation for the Kingdom of Scotland, based on the solid rock of faith provided by Peter's brother, supported fervently by all the estates and kings of Scotland, centred on what would become the See of St Andrews.

St Rule gathers about him men and women of holy life to make the momentous journey – St Damian, a priest; Gelasius and Chubaculus, deacons; Merniacus the brother of St Damian; Nerius and Elrisenius from Crete; Mirenus, Machabeus and Silvius his brother. There were also eight hermits – Felix, Sajanus, Matheus, Mauricius, Madianus, Philip, Luke and Eugenius – and three virgin saints from Colsoia, Triduana, Potencia and Emerea.

After a voyage of nearly two years, sailing without charts or knowing where their final destination was – beyond the Pillars of Hercules (the Straits of Gibraltar), Rule's ship is finally caught by a powerful wind and smashed onto the rocks of the kingdom of the Picts.

There are two further strands to the St Andrew legend in Scotland: around the year AD 800 Angus, King of Picts offers a tenth of his kingdom to St Andrew in return for the miraculous help he was given at the Battle of Athelstaneford. In an apparently unconnected episode, St Rule dies 32 years after his arrival in Fife. Both versions of the foundation story seem to have been drawn from related, if not identical sources. St Rule (French Rieul) is thought to be a confusion with St Regulus of Senlis in France. There was a church of St Andrew at Senlis and he was said to have come from Greece to Gaul in the fourth century. Late-medieval calendars celebrate the Scottish Regulus on the same day as Regulus of Senlis (30 March) and also on that of an Irish St Riaguil of Mucc-Inis in Lochderg (16 October) who was active at Kilrymont around AD 580. It might be that Regulus, the bringer of St Andrew's relics to Scotland was a pious literary fiction, but the fiction may have been grafted onto an existing local cult.

It can be seen that in the legend of the Battle of Athelstaneford and in that of St Rule, the hand which is seen as governing the development and outcome of the story is God's. Both Angus and Rule are totally free agents, but they do not have the ability to shape their future without the divine intervention of St Andrew or the angel. Like Constantine at the Milvian Bridge, defeat for Angus means almost certain death. Similarly, Rule sails from Patras in fear of his life, only doing so because the angel makes him an offer he cannot refuse.

If Rule's pioneering voyage is carefully grafted into the chronicle of an Irish saint called Riaguil or a French saint called Rieul, he also has two other functions. He bypasses the unpalatable fact that the relics of Andrew came through the intermediary of English or England-based missionaries and he acts as a compressed, disguised and semi-fictionalised version of actual historical events.

It should be emphasised that neither St Regulus nor Acca were the first to establish a Christian foundation at Kilrymont. There was a monastery there before Regulus landed or Acca left Hexham. In AD 747 the Irish annals of Tigernach record the death of Tuathalain, Abbot of Cinrighmonaid (Kilrymont or Kinrymont).

Sixteenth-century wooden Burgh Arms of St Andrews. (Courtesy of Fife Council Museums)

Legend also relates that at Kilrymont there stood an ancient pagan sacred grove of oak trees. It is said that when Christians first came to the site, in accordance with the policy of Pope Gregory, the Great Tree was carefully dismembered and parts of it incorporated into the rafters of the first Christian church. Later, the oak tree came to feature on the medieval seals of the town of St Andrews.

Being too complex, the ramifications of the true story of how Andrew's body came to Patras, to Constantinople, to Rome and to Hexham may have been compressed and telescoped by the chronicler Walter Bower and his fellow Augustinian predecessors into a striking and memorable fable. This fable preserves an important and highly diplomatic kernel of truth – that the Church of the Picts (and subsequently of the Scots) had authentic roots in the teaching of Christ and his Apostles.

7

Andrew the Saint

AS NUMEROUS REFERENCES IN PAPAL correspondence and archaeological research testify, the major pilgrimage centres in the world were Jerusalem, Rome and Compostela in Spain. The only religious centres outside the fringes of the Mediterranean which could claim to possess major corporeal relics of an Apostle were the shrines of St James in Compostela, of St Matthias in Trier (Germany) and of St Andrew in Fife. The Dark Ages were rife with foundation legends. Rival places of pilgrimage vied with each other as economic considerations took priority over the egalitarian vision of the Community of Saints. Local pride and imagination often attributed spurious antiquity to a shrine or alleged its foundation by New Testament figures in order to increase status and boost tourism.

A church in Marseilles, for example, was said to have been founded by Lazarus and his sisters, another in Mantua by Longinus (the soldier who pierced Christ's side on Calvary). Glastonbury in England claimed Joseph of Arimathea as its founder. In Paris it was Dionysius the Areopagite. St Andrews, however, was significantly different. There, no attempt was made to attribute its foundation to a known personage from the pages of the New Testament. Moreover, the supposed founder, Regulus, functions as a storyteller's symbol. He is the convincing and dramatic adhesive which papers over the cracks in a truncated and sanitised version of real events.

Early in its history, the shrine of the Apostle at Kilrymont was able to attract widespread aristocratic respect. The *Prophecy of Berchan* (an 11th-century poem) tells of several kings and princes ending their days as pilgrims or religious in 'the home of the Apostle at the boundary of the breakers'. King Constantine II of Alba, son of Aed, abdicated and retired to monastic life at St Andrews in AD c.943, where he died as its abbot in AD 952. His son, Indulf, passed away 'in the house of the same holy Apostle' ten years later. Another Aed, son of Maelmithid (an Irish royal prince), is recorded as having died at St Andrews in AD 965 while on pilgrimage

The foundation legends describe how, in addition to the main basilica dedicated to St Andrew, seven other chapels were built on the headland over the harbour. These would have been small buildings, probably constructed largely of wood.

The original monastic foundation which existed when the relics of Andrew came to Kilrymont, would have been Celtic, the fruit of many missionary initiatives from Ireland. The Celtic monks, following a rule and largely concerned with their own community's life of prayer, were to be succeeded in later centuries by the Culdees (known in the time of King James IV as 'Irish monks'). They co-existed, sometimes uneasily, as stubbornly unregenerated religious communities within the mainstream ecclesiastical structure.

The Culdees had begun as an eighth-century reforming movement of Irish monks. Their rule of living encouraged strict observance of the sabbath and forbade the use of alcohol or music. However, their sacred literature, illuminated manuscripts and work in precious metals was exquisitely imaginative and colourful. At *Cill Rìmhinn* (Kilrymont) the Culdees were a community which also served the religious needs of the local people. In later centuries they were hereditary priests, living a largely secular life which appears to have permitted them to marry. A Culdee community was probably fully established at St Andrews by around the AD 950.

In the tenth century, a frequent pilgrim to the shrine of Andrew was St Godric of Finchale, who referred to it as 'the far-famed house of St Andrew'. For his contemporary, the author of the life of St Cadoc, it seemed highly appropriate for St Cadoc to round off pilgrimages to Jerusalem and Rome with a visit to the basilica of the Apostle Andrew in Fife.

Evidence of the growing importance of the shrine is also found in a magnificent Pictish sandstone sarcophagus, one of 66 Pictish sculptured stones found near the cathedral, dating from the ninth century which was unearthed on the site in 1833.[21] Framed between interlaced Celtic ornamentation, the central figure is that of David pulling apart the jaws of a lion while armed men hunt rabbits and deer through a wood (perhaps Swine Wood – Muckross, or in Latin *cursus apri*).

The church now known as St Rule's was constructed around 1070. It was designed as a reliquary church whose tall square tower (over 100 feet in height) would perform much the same function as the Statue of Liberty in New York – acting as a guide and landmark for pilgrims approaching by land or sea. But by 1124, it became clear to King Alexander I that, in addition to constructing a larger and more appropriate church, something would have to be done to place the

St Rule's Tower, St Andrews.
(Author's copyright)

staffing of the shrine on a more permanent basis – there was no resident priest from the secular clergy and the shrine was served only by a handful of the increasingly idiosyncratic Culdees who by this time celebrated Mass according to rites no longer widely in use, but they still expected to receive a hereditary share of church revenue. Regular weekly services or services on special occasions were not easily available to monarch or people.

Only a few months before his death in 1124, Alexander arranged for Robert, prior of his Augustinian community at Scone, to be elected bishop at St Andrews. However, it was not until 20 years later (after many legal and practical difficulties) that Bishop Robert, with the support of King David I (1124-53), was finally able to endow a priory of Augustinian canons at St Andrews which would become the most important church corporation in Scotland.

From the time of David royal ordinance decreed that those on pilgrimage should enjoy the King's Peace (a forerunner of the modern passport):

> Those men that are on pilgrimage and are visiting holy
> places for their souls' health, shall have our firm peace
> in going and coming, so that no man does them wrong
> provided they behave lawfully.

Royal protection was also extended in the case of those in trouble with the law:

> If a man is away on pilgrimage to Jerusalem, St James or
> Rome, an accusation against him should be suspended
> until his return.

The Laws of the Burghs echoed this ruling:

> If any man from the King's burgh go on pilgrimage with
> permission of the Church and his neighbours, to the

> Holy Land or to St James or to any other holy place for
> the health of his soul, his house and his household shall
> be in our Lord the King's peace and in the bailies' until
> God bring him home again.

For pilgrims venturing abroad, there were fixed limits on the length
of their absence: England (three weeks); Paris, St Denis (seven weeks);
Rome and St James (16 weeks); Jerusalem (one year).

Among the notable Scots who went on pilgrimage abroad was the
14th-century soldier, Alexander Lyndesy, described as *justiciar* north
of the Forth. Sadly he died on the island of Candia while on his way
to Jerusalem. Normally, permission to go on pilgrimage had to be
obtained from the king. Members of the Scottish aristocracy also
went on pilgrimage. In December 1499 leave was granted to Robert,
Lord Lyle to go on pilgrimage. Nine years later, Patrick, Lord Lindsay
of Kirkforther was given royal protection for his pilgrimage.

A colourful but exaggerated, description of a typical Scottish pilgrim is preserved in a late 12th-century chronicle connected with the
Abbey of Bury St Edmunds. Abbot Sampson of Bury, records the
chronicler, decided he had to go to Rome to ensure a suitable an
appointment to the now vacant church at Woolpit. Because it was the
time of the schism between Pope Alexander III and Pope Octavian
(1159-64), the abbot was terrified of being imprisoned in Italy or of
being mutilated and tortured by the opponents of the pope. He
decided to travel to Rome disguised as a Scots pilgrim. He dressed
himself up as a tramp, with ragged clothes, leggings and breeches and
carried a pair of old shoes over his shoulders. He would shake his
walking-staff violently at people who made fun of him, using threatening language 'after the manner of the Scots'. In his little wallet he
carried a small jug for drinking. In spite of all these precautions, the
abbot was robbed just outside Rome. He lost all his money and was
only able to return to England
by begging from door to door!

By the 11th and 12th cen-
turies, pilgrimages to St
Andrews were sufficiently frequent and substantial to war-
rant the opening of two ferry
services across the Firth of
Forth, supported by hostels on
both shores. Within the shrine

Ruins of the 12th-century St Andrew's Church near
the harbour, North Berwick. (Author's copyright)

community itself, a hostel now also existed which could cater for guests. There were two main routes to St Andrews. Founded in the middle of the 12th century by Duncan, fourth earl of Fife (and granted by his sons and heirs to the nuns of North Berwick), the longer ferry crossing from North Berwick on the south bank of the Firth of Forth to Ardross in Fife was known as the Earl's Ferry. It was supported by hostels at both harbours. For bona fide pilgrims, passage on the ferry was free. A 13th-century stone mould for mass-producing pilgrim's signs was unearthed in North Berwick in the 19th century. Its design shows St Andrew on his cross.

Pewter Pilgrim Badge of St Andrew. (Courtesy of Fife Council Museums)

Further west was the older and better known Queen's Ferry. It had been founded by Queen Margaret and also provided hostels on either shore. Later monarchs – David I, Malcolm IV, William the Lion, and Alexander II, all upheld the right of pilgrims to use the ferries free of charge. Bishop Malvoisin of St Andrews (1202-38) founded a hospice around 1214 at Scotlandwell, an ancient healing well near Loch Leven, for pilgrims and other needy persons.

When pilgrims reached the north shore of the Firth of Forth, they would travel through Cupar by the royal highway to St Andrews. Pilgrims arriving from the north-east of Scotland would cross the Firth of Tay from Taum in the ferry boat managed by the priory of St Andrews.

The bridge over the River Eden at Guardbridge just outside St Andrews was a *statio* (a halting-place and assembly point) on the pilgrim route. Around 1419, Bishop Henry Wardlaw started to build the stone structure which can still be seen today, the original wooden bridge having disappeared, after being swept away in a flash flood which drowned a group of priests on pilgrimage.

As early as the 1150s, in preparation for the construction of the new cathedral church, Bishop Robert had his town planners and engineers lay out two wide streets which converged towards the ecclesiastical centre of the town at the east. Medieval St Andrews seemed specifically designed to provide a circular route for solemn public processions (via North and South Streets), leaving the centre street itself free for booths and stalls (in Market Street) where later, merchants and itinerant showmen provided food, trade and entertainment. It

Statio at Guardbridge. (Courtesy of Jurek Pütter)

might almost seem as if St Andrews had been planned according to the design of a pilgrim's scallop-shell – radiating streets converging into the shrine, or fingers of a hand.

Ruins of St Andrews Cathedral, St Andrews.
(Author's copyright)

Under Robert's successor, Bishop Arnold, foundation work on the future cathedral church began in 1160 to the north-west of St Rule's tower. In 1199 Pope Innocent III granted a licence to the bishop to build a new and larger church to meet the increase in the population of the parish at St Andrews. As the building slowly progressed so did news of a new development for the bones of St Andrew and our focus now moves from Scotland to Italy, to the Gulf of Salerno and the picturesque coastal town of Amalfi, some 62 kilometres south of Naples.

An independent republic from the seventh century until 1075, Amalfi was an important port and later became one of the principal Norman posts. Amalfi had easy communications with the East from earliest times: Gregory the Great, writing in AD 596, makes earliest reference to the Christian community at Amalfi which had its first bishop in that year and which became an archbishopric in AD 987. In later years, the Archdiocese of Amalfi became directly dependent on the Holy See.

Until AD 839 Amalfi had belonged to the Byzantine duchy of Naples. After that date, the city and its territory became an independent state within the orbit of the Byzantine Empire. From the ninth century, many Amalfitans were active in Mediterranean trade. Between 1055-

Modern-day Amalfi. (Author's copyright)

1062 Amalfi tried in vain to organise an alliance of the West and East empires as a defence against the Norman invaders of southern Italy. Amalfi's traffic with the East is reflected in its architecture. The magnificent doors of the Duomo (cathedral) Sant'Andrea, for example, were commissioned by the head of the Amalfi colony in Constantinople and were constructed there in 1066 before being shipped over to Italy.

The Cathedral of Sant' Andrea, Amalfi.
(Author's copyright)

A new player in the story of St Andrew is an Amalfi-born papal legate, Bishop Peter Capuano who, while on a mission to Palestine, had learned of the capture and sack of Constantinople by the French Crusaders and travelled to join them in the city. There, in the church of Hagia Sophia, at a conference with clergy of the Greek rite in December 1204, he demanded that the Greeks conform to Roman liturgical practice. Capuano, aware of the importance of the vast quantity of religious objects in Constantinople, set about gathering together many relics of the saints – the bodies of Andrew (from the church of the Holy Apostles), of Cosmas and Damian, Vitus and the hermit Macarius. In March 1206, Capuano, guarding his relics, arrived with a fleet of nine galleys at the port of Gaeta to the north of Naples and proceeded to transfer them to Amalfi.

Two years later, during the night of 7 May 1208, the body of the Apostle was given a place of honour in the city, with candles and incense burning, venerated by large numbers of the people. At day-break, the sun shone over Amalfi. The city had been newly decorated, hung with coloured cloths and sprinkled with masses of flowers. A great crowd singing hymns and carrying candles, went to meet the body. The bishops, the Archbishop of Amalfi and the (by this time) Cardinal Capuano came forward barefooted to lift the coffin of St Andrew onto their shoulders. Then they carried it solemnly into the cathedral, where the Cardinal preached to the people, asking them to honour the body of the Apostle by the worthiness of their lives. He opened the coffin of the Apostle, reverently showing the head and the other bones one at a time to the applauding crowd. The relics were immediately taken down into the crypt and placed in a silver container covered by a large slab of marble upon which the high altar was constructed. The Apostle's bones would not be seen again for many years.

In fact, the relics were divided into two portions and buried in separate places, the skull being put in the least accessible location. Undoubtedly, the intention was to protect the relics from those who might wish to take the body back to Constantinople. Eight years later, Pope Honorius III asked the Chapter (the canons or ruling body) of Amalfi Cathedral to release the relics of Andrew to Rome. The Chapter, however, refused to give up any part of the relics, saying they did not know exactly where they had been hidden.

* * *

That year (1216) coincidentally, is also the date of the papal bull of Honorius III which confirmed the constitutional basis of the Scottish Church – the *Ecclesia Scoticana*. This had already been established in 1192 by Pope Celestine III's bull *Cum universi* which placed the Scottish church under the Holy See as a 'special daughter' ('*filia specialis*') without any intermediate authority.

From as early as the 12th century, the papacy had noted the unwavering loyalty of Scottish monarchs to the Christian faith and to Rome. Queen Margaret, with her ecclesiastical reforms, and her son

David I, with his widespread introduction of new monastic orders into Scotland and his foundation of Scottish abbeys, made Scotland (from a papal perspective) in many respects a model kingdom. But, in spite of his great missionary zeal, David failed to win the one concession from the papacy that would have meant more than all the rest – the conferring of archi-Episcopal rank upon the ancient see of St Andrews.

Both York and Canterbury tried to control the Scottish Church but it was not until the pontificate of Rolando Bandinelli (Pope Alexander III, 1159-81) that any substantial advance was made to protect the Scottish church from its predatory English neighbours. In 1182 Alexander's successor, Pope Lucius, gave King Malcolm IV's brother, William the Lion, a mark of special favour – the Golden Rose. Pope Urban III (1185-7) recognised the church (ie the diocese) of Glasgow as a 'special daughter' of Rome, without any intermediate authority. Celestine III (1191-8) extended this close dependence to the entire Scottish Church, except for the bishoprics of Galloway (which remained under the archbishop of York) and the Scottish Isles and Orkney (at that time within the Norwegian province of Trondheim).

As well as confirming Celestine III's *Cum universi*, Honorius III also gave Scots clergy the right to hold regular councils presided over by a specially appointed bishop. For Scotland, the papacy was the ultimate spiritual court of appeal and, when necessary, the court of first instance. On matters of great importance, special papal envoys (*legates*) would be sent to Scotland to conduct affairs on behalf of the papacy.

During the campaigns of Charles Martel against the Saracens in the eighth century, the whereabouts of the cross of St Andrew from Patras had been lost, but in the year 1250, it was re-discovered at the monastery of St Victoire at Weaune, near Marseilles in France. Legend had it that the cross was given by the Burgundians to the monastery in the first century AD. A small portion of it, preserved intact in a silver case, had been taken by Philip, Duke of Burgundy to Brussels where, in 1429, he formed the Order of the Golden Fleece whose badge is the saltire or Cross of Burgundy.[22] There were also connections between Burgundy and Scotland.[23] In 1497 Pedro de Ayala, Spanish ambassador to Scotland, wrote to Ferdinand and Isabella of Spain that the Dukes of Burgundy wore the saltire of St Andrew in memory of help which Scotland had once given Burgundy. Most of the original relic was finally destroyed in 1793.

In the 13th and 14th centuries, Scotland was forced to defend itself against the ambitions of Edward I of England and his son Edward II. Edward I, claiming overlordship of Scotland, had a seal made in 1291 with the figure of St Andrew upon it and it was the political correctness of a very astute kind that arranged for Edward's choice as King of Scotland – John Balliol – to be inaugurated on St Andrew's Day, 1292.

However, in this struggle to survive as an independent nation, Scotland received notable support from Pope Boniface VIII, who, in his letter *Scimus, fili* (1300), commanded Edward to end his incursions north of the Border. Scotland, asserted Boniface, belonged to the Holy See because it had been miraculously converted to the Christian faith by the relics of St Andrew. Tradition has it that when the Archbishop of Canterbury delivered the pope's letter to Edward at Sweetheart Abbey, he was almost too apprehensive to face the king.

In the very same year, the next episode in the story of the Apostle Andrew took place in Amalfi. The less important parts of his body (not the skull) were also unexpectedly found in the silver container under the high altar in which Cardinal Capuano had had them buried almost a century before. But it was to be another 300 years before the other parts of his body (including the skull) were discovered in the same church.

8
Relics and Politics

IT WAS NOT UNTIL 5 July 1318 that the consecration of the new St Andrews Cathedral took place, on a windy headland in Fife. Probably the actual rituale (order of service) used at the consecration was the Pontifical of Bishop David Bernham – now in the Bibliothèque Nationale, Paris – which had been used during the 13th century by the bishops of St Andrews, David Bernham and William Wishart.

In the presence of seven bishops, 15 abbots and most of the nobility of Scotland, King Robert the Bruce, representing the people of Scotland, added to the traditional liturgy of consecration by announcing an annual endowment towards the upkeep of the cathedral of 100 merks sterling as thanksgiving for the victory at Bannockburn four years earlier.

This consecration of a church in gratitude for victory in war is an almost unprecedented event in medieval Europe. King Robert divided the spoils of Bannockburn among the churches of Scotland. Among other trophies, the new St Andrews Cathedral received a cross of rock crystal, and it is probable that two statues (of the Virgin Mary and St Andrew) were placed in the cathedral by the Douglas family about the same time.

With a total interior area of 2,415sq m/2,888sq ft and an interior length of 108 metres, the cathedral was the visible evidence of a renewed national Church. The interior length of its nave was smaller than Canterbury (157m/515ft), York (148m/486ft), Durham (121m/397ft) or the medieval basilica of St Peter, Rome (122m/400ft). However, it was larger than that of Aeneas Sylvius Piccolomini's home Cathedral of Siena (97m/318ft) and those of Santiago de Compostela (96m/315ft), Glasgow (86m/282ft) or Amalfi (57m/187ft).

The national Church's credibility rested on the few small pieces of bone which were believed to have come from the body of the Apostle. As John Patrick Crichton-Stuart, 3rd Marquess of Bute, was to remark many centuries later (1894), when delivering his rectorial address at St Andrews University:

Whatever the history of these bits of bone, and whether they were or were not part of the body of the first-called Apostle of Christ, they were undoubtedly believed at the time to be genuine, and they were the immediate cause of the creation of St Andrews as the great national church of Scotland.

It was a sumptuous interior that visitors walking across the orange terracotta tiles of the cathedral nave could see. The brightly painted statues were laden with valuable offerings. North and south of the high altar were the principal images of the Virgin Mary and St Andrew whose votive lamps were maintained by the Douglas family. On feast days, a magnificent red carpet covered the floor of the sanctuary.

On the altar were velvet cushion book-rests and silver-gilt cruets held the water and wine. Holy water would be scattered over the congregation using a brush with a silver

John Patrick Crichton-Stuart,
3rd Marquess of Bute (1847-1900)

handle. Behind the altar, there was probably a painted triptych. This would have rivalled in quality the Trinity Altarpiece (with its panel depicting James III protected by St Andrew) commissioned for the charitable foundation of Trinity College, Edinburgh by Edward Bonkil and executed by the Ghent artist, Hugo van der Goes (died 1482).

Only the most privileged pilgrims would penetrate into the innermost Chapel of the Relics where the bones of St Andrew were enshrined beyond the wooden screen in front of the high altar, housed in a relict *aumbry* (relic recess) in the centre of the chapel, built high enough to be seen by the rest of the congregation over the wooden screen. In front of the shrine was an altar. Around the walls were the other reliquaries and other treasures of the church.

Security was a major consideration. Few medieval inventory of relics and treasures survive, but we do know that in addition to the reliquary containing the bones of Andrew, there were other jewels such as the silver shaft of King Alexander I (1077-1124) which had been made into a processional cross. There were 40cm-long tusks of ancient boars from the 'Boar's Raik'. They were fixed by small chains to the choir stalls. Another treasure was the crystal cross taken from the field of Bannockburn. The bones of St Andrew were not enshrined as separate relics, but were all housed in one reliquary. This was observed by the English chronicler, John Hardyng, who visited St Andrews in the early 15th century. The reliquary would have been made by craftsman of the Celtic era and like other reliquaries of that period, it had a traditional Celtic name.

Just as the crosier-reliquary of St Fillan was called the 'Quigrich', and the enshrined psalter of St Columba known as the 'Cathach', so the reliquary of St Andrew was 'Morbrac' (the Great Reliquary), from the Gaelic *breac* meaning 'bright' (because of its precious metals and multi-coloured enameling) and *mor* meaning 'great'.

At the beginning of the 13th century, the designation 'Morbrac' is to be found in an agreement drawn up over the lands of Scoonie and Garriach, in which a certain Gellin, son of Gillecrist Maccusseger is guaranteed by the canons of St Andrews that he will have the privilege of carrying the Morbrac just as Gillemur his predecessor formerly did, and will have the emoluments of food and clothing which his predecessor had enjoyed. The principal public appearances of the Morbrac were when it was carried in solemn procession through the town.

There is little detailed information about these processions; there would be one on the principal feast of St Andrew – Andermass, on the 30 November. But Walter Bower tells us that there was also a procession on 6 February when the feast of the *Translation* (arrival) of the relics was celebrated.

In preparation for the procession, the streets of the town would be scrupulously cleaned at public expense. The trade guilds would provide static religious tableaux and pageant actors who walked in the procession. The masters and scholars of the colleges would hold flowers and leafy branches. The Blackfriars and the Greyfriars took part, as would the Culdee canons of the Chapel Royal of St Mary of the Rock. The Augustinian canons took pride of place near the reliquary. They would wear the finest vestments chosen from the cathedral sacristy, with garlands of flowers or jewelled bands around their heads.

Before the procession, the base of the house-shaped reliquary carrier would be inserted during solemn High Mass into square slot holes in the middle of the chancel (still visible today). The Morbrac, with its base mounted on a wooden stretcher covered by a canopy, would be carried either by the canons of the cathedral or by prominent laymen. In the procession, hymns would be sung and the bells of the cathedral and the other town churches would ring out. After dusk, bonfires were lit and fireworks set off into the night sky.

Walter Bower quotes an inscription on a votive offering that listed the nationalities who came to St Andrews – Franks, Normans, Flemings, Teutons, English, Germans, Dutch, French, Italians – many combining trade with piety.

Square slot holes in the chancel of St Andrews Cathedral. (Author's copyright)

The St Andrews-based historical illustrator, Jurek Pütter, conjectures what would have happened as the pilgrims arrived at the shrine of the Apostle:

> The Morbrac is covered with a very large, comparatively unadorned black box in the shape of a house. When people were ushered in to the darkened reliquary chamber (a lot of these events were conducted in the evening) several small candles were lit, just enough to reveal the mysterious appearance of the black box. As more candles were lit you had the Augustinians beginning the first liturgical rites, solemn prayers, then the box would start to be raised. As it's raised, the cables holding the box have trips on them, so that as the cable rises up, it trips the bells. It's like a musical box. What you had was the tremendous visual spectacle of an enormous black box being lifted up to reveal the glittering ornament of the reliquary underneath. Candles and oil lamps would be progressively lit whilst all this is going on. This is a standard device.

According to Pütter, the black reliquary box (constructed to follow the house shape of the Morbrac), was lightly constructed so that it didn't have too great a weight. It could be hand-cranked up into position from behind the screens in such a way that the pilgrims couldn't see the mechanism, so there was a sense of utter mystery. The black box was always unadorned, the design of the apparatus using the skill of the illusionist – in the dark, the box was perfectly invisible. The whole process created a wonderful sense of mystery and peace for the pilgrim entering the richly decorated reliquary chamber. Pütter again:

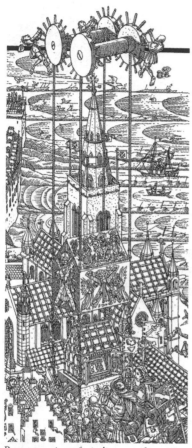

Reconstruction of winding gear for raising the roof of the St Andrews reliquary (Courtesy of Jurek Pütter)

The one thing that stood out was the black box. It would have been enormous. Maybe eight or nine feet long; six feet wide; maybe as much as six to seven feet high. When it was lifted, inside it would have been painted a dark blue with silver stars, so that, as it rose, you could see a cosmos revealed. It's still a favourite device used in Spain, Portugal and Italy from the later Middle Ages and the Renaissance period.

As musical instruments and mechanical devices improved, then you had great revivals in reliquary shrines as new technology was used to heighten further the impact. The New World, Mexico, the whole of South America where you have these devotional shrines, still make use of similar devices.

The reliquary chamber could maybe take 40 to 50 people at a time, but pilgrims were not permitted to enter into the shrine unattended or unsupervised. From the time when thefts and public disorder were at their height, the Augustinian canons, who were the church authorities in St Andrews, would only allow special guests to view the relics close up. By and large the average pilgrim could come into the reliquary chamber and be treated to this unique experience but it wasn't a spectacle that was available simply on demand. It was a controlled, arranged spectacle, simply

because of theft, of damage, because of over-emotional-
ism or the possibility of hysteria.

The typical pilgrim did catch sight of the relics but they were never
permitted to touch them or get close to them. The only time the
Morbrac was moved out of the cathedral was on feast days.

The effect of pilgrimage on the size of the local population could
be dramatic, so all pilgrim towns had their population capped.
Pilgrim towns were not permitted to grow beyond their capacity to
sustain both their indigenous population and the influx of pilgrims.

While the emphasis was on pilgrims, not on the town's population,
the authorities worked to a mathematical equation. There was no
point in advertising pilgrimages throughout the whole of Christian
Europe, if at the end of the day, they couldn't be fed. Feeding people
was more important than housing them, because in summer months
you could still camp outside. Jurek Pütter points out:

> It was of paramount importance that people were fed, if
> they were an international pilgrim in residence for two
> to three months. Towns like Dunfermline were fixed at
> a population of about two thousand; St Andrews to
> about five thousand. It never grew – it was not permit-
> ted to grow.

In 1997, Nick Haplin, then a Dundee University student counsellor,
commented:

> St Andrews was really a service city. Its most lucrative
> activity was the great bed-and-breakfast industry. It had
> the ability to accommodate additional thousands, espe-
> cially at the high summer months of the year. That was
> how much of the city's wealth was generated.

To accommodate the pilgrims 'stations' or stopping-places were constructed. The pilgrim station at Guardbridge was between 60 to 90
metres across. Its dormitory could accommodate, at its last development, about 200 people. In the evenings the refectory was converted
to a dormitory. In the warm summer months the pilgrims just lived
in tents in the courtyard. Earlshall Castle nearby was probably largely
constructed for Sir William Bruce in 1546 using stone taken from the
demolished station. When Sir Robert Lorimer came to restore the

Pilgrimage to St Andrews.
(Courtesy of Jurek Pütter)

castle in the late 19th century, he designed a stone gateway in the garden which is surmounted by a scallop shell, the ancient pilgrims' badge, as if to remind the casual visitor of St Andrews' long association with pilgrimage.

The real value of a pilgrimage was the physical journey. Edward I of England had a particular interest in pilgrimages. In 1270, two years before he became king, he had established a fine reputation as a knight on the Eighth (and last) Crusade. Three years later, safe-passage to go on pilgrimage to St Andrews was granted on behalf of King Edward (who did not return to England for his coronation till 1274), to three Englishmen – Richard, son of Philip; Lawrence Scot and Nicholas de Wygenhale.

The most detailed account of an ordinary pilgrim's visit to St Andrews and his motivation for it, is to be found in the story of William Bondolf, a cleric and burger of Dunkirk (possibly an Englishman), who had killed Andrieu d'Esquerdes (perhaps a Scot named Andrew Kerr – from the Scots word corrie for 'left'). Bondolf was ordered to pay a fine of 12 livres, to have 13 masses sung for the soul of the deceased and to make the pilgrimage to St Andrews – presumably because the victim was Scottish. On 29 May 1333, Bondolf completed his pilgrimage and received a certificate and seal of authentication from John of Gowrie, prior of St Andrews. By 26 June 1333 Bondolf was back in France at Saint-Omer where he presented his certificate and received absolution for his crime.

St Andrew could also be invoked for protection from disease. The English chronicler Thomas Walsingham (who died about 1422) records a prayer used by the Scots in 1379, which asked God and St Andrew to shield them from the pestilence, 'the foul death that Englishmen dien [die] upon'.

A red-letter day for the Fife town came on 3 February 1414 when St Andrews University was formally founded. In the procession on 6

February to mark this momentous event, some 400 clerics joined with a host of layfolk.

In the late autumn of 1435, an Italian scholar and diplomat, Aeneas Silvius Piccolomini (then still technically a layman as he was only in Minor Orders and not yet ordained a priest), was sent by Cardinal Niccolò Albergati, a papal diplomat working for Pope Eugene IV, on an undercover mission from Avignon to Scotland with orders to persuade James I of Scotland to launch an attack on England and so help end the Hundred Years' war with France. A secondary aim of Piccolomini's covert mission was to restore the status of Scottish archdeacon William Croyser who had been condemned for treason and deprived of his office in the papal courts at Florence. Preparing to cross over to England, in the autumn of 1435, Siena-born Piccolomini was first arrested at Calais and later released. On his way to London to see his close friend, the Englishman Adam de Molin, senior secretary to the Avignon papacy, Piccolomini visited the shrine of St Thomas à Becket at Canterbury. In his memoirs, written almost 30 years later from notes made in his own diaries, Piccolomini speaks with awe of the gilded mausoleum of Thomas which glittered with diamonds, pearls and carbuncles. On another occasion he declared himself to be full of admiration at the stained-glass windows in York Minster, which he saw, probably in 1436, on his journey south from Scotland.

To reach London, Piccolomini would have passed through Rochester, famous for its shrine of St Andrew. However, in spite of the efforts of his friend de Molin, Piccolomini was refused permission to travel overland to the Scottish Border. Frustrated once more, he returned to the Continent, going first to Bruges in Belgium and then Sluys. From Sluys, he and his servants set sail for Scotland – perhaps aiming for St Andrews, the permanent religious and administrative centre of the country – in contrast to the peripatetic royal court of James I, which moved regularly with the monarch between several Scottish locations.

Many years later, writing of himself as he was at that time – a cultivated diplomat of 30, the 60-year old Pius II, tells his story in the third person:

> Then he took ship for Scotland, but was driven towards
> Norway by two violent gales, one of which kept them in
> fear of death for fourteen hours.

Piccolomini describes himself and his sailing companions as being totally disoriented and at the mercy of the elements as they headed towards what he believed to be a deprived and culturally barren nation:

> The other gale pounded the ship for two nights and a
> day, so that she sprang a leak and was carried so far out
> to sea toward the north that the sailors, who could no
> longer read the constellations, abandoned all hope.

He then rationalises his adventures by turning them into a parable with a moral:

> But the Divine mercy came to their aid, raising north
> winds, which drove the vessel back toward the mainland
> and finally on the twelfth day brought them in sight of
> Scotland.

The ship, still taking in water, manages to limp into port, probably Belhaven,close to Dunbar in East Lothian:

> When they had made harbour, Aeneas, in fulfilment of
> a vow, walked barefoot to the nearest shrine.

To get to the nearest shrine (fragments of which have been recently discovered by archaeologists), Aeneas would have to cross the Peffer Burn which, as the Cogtail Burn, runs all the way from Athelstaneford.[24] He walked five miles to 'the holy well at Whitekirk dedicated to the Virgin Mary'. Even after the Reformation, the custom of 'creeping' to Whitekirk continued. Piccolomini recalled that:

> After resting there for two hours, he found on rising
> that he could not walk a step, his feet were so weak and
> numb with the cold. It was his salvation that there was
> nothing there to eat and he had to go on to another vil-
> lage.

It is possible that the second village he visited was North Berwick:

> While he was being carried there by his servants, Aeneas
> warmed up his feet by continuously banging them on

the ground. Against all expectation, he recovered and was able to walk again.

However, as a result of this mortification of walking five miles over frozen ground, Piccolomini was to suffer from rheumatism for the rest of his life.

However, these statements based on notes in his diary written many years before, Piccolomini's account is selective and cannot always be entirely trusted as it was written when he would have his dignity as pope to consider. He implies that he fulfilled his mission (of which he says nothing), in that he met the king – where, we are not told, (in Edinburgh or perhaps Perth) – and spent some seven months in Scotland, all told.

In the Piccolomini Library in Aeneas's home town of Siena, the painter Pinturicchio's imaginative portrait of King James of 1505-8, with its exotic interpretation of the Scottish landscape, does little to shed light on the events of his visit to Scotland. But it is tempting to see in the coastal city far behind the king's head, a representation of St Andrews with its fortified walls, towers and steeples.

In spite of all his efforts, Piccolomini was not able to provoke James into attacking England as he had hoped. The Scots king proved himself immovable in spite of all Aeneas' attempts to persuade him otherwise. Perhaps this explains Aeneas' uncharacteristic description of the Scots king in his *Commentaries* as being squat and thickset. James, a patron of the arts and author of the collection of poems known as *The Kingis Quair*, had been a prisoner of the English for 18 years. He had been educated in England and, having a fine physique, even fought for Henry V at Agincourt in France. During his reign in Scotland, James placed considerable importance on finance and law and order. In his relations with the Church, however, he was abrasive. This may partly explain his assassination, two years after Aeneas' visit, at the Dominican friary in Perth.

James' response to Aeneas' mission was to refuse to declare war on England, but he did promise not to provide assistance to the English. Although James did not reinstate archdeacon William Croyser, he observed the niceties of diplomacy by reimbursing Aeneas for his travelling expenses and giving him money and two horses for his return journey through England.

Writing in April 1436 to his patron, Cardinal Albergati, Aeneas excuses himself for not having communicated with him during the seven long and painful months he had endured the Scottish climate and culture. He indicates that Scotland was economically and cultural-ly depressed, that he had no means of getting a private letter out of the country and adds that in any case no developments took place during his stay which could remotely assist Albergati's political goals. Scotland, according to Piccolomini's official report, was of little importance.

Nevertheless, in a later account of Scotland contained in his *Commentaries* and the brief geographical notes included in his *Europa* (1453), Aeneas gives a version of his Scottish mission which is quite the reverse of this tight-lipped, damage-limitation correspondence which attempts to gloss over the failure of his mission. His hidden agenda, as an ambitious young man, was to persuade Albergati of the hardships he had had to endure in Scotland in faithfully carrying out his master's instructions.

By contrast, in his *Commentaries* Aeneas the Renaissance human-ist takes care to paint a bizarre, arresting picture of the idiosyncrasies of a cold and far-off nation which burned black stones as fuel and had geese growing from trees. Here he makes use of the tradition of trav-el-writing popularised by the 14th-century *Voyage of Sir John Mandeville*, a guide for pilgrims to the Holy Land which combined geography, natural history, romance and marvels.

Nine years later, in a letter to his father, Piccolomini reveals yet another motive for sanitising his true experiences north of the Border and his seven months stay in the country: he had fathered a son by a Scots woman, but the child evidently died after a few years of life.

Knowing Aeneas's interest in the shrine at Canterbury, it is unthinkable that, during his time in Scotland, he would not have crossed to Fife and on to the metropolitan cathedral at St Andrews where, as a high-ranking ecclesiastical emissary, he would have paid his respects to Bishop Henry Wardlaw. However, despite the high probability of a visit to the shrine of the Apostle, Aeneas is intriguing-ly silent about the relics at St Andrews.

Twenty years after his visit to Scotland, Piccolomini spent some time touring near Naples. He went to Baiae and Cumae (where Aeneas had been taken by the Sibyl to the nether world and whose prophecies the Emperor Maxentius had consulted before the Battle of Milvian Bridge). Piccolomini went to Salerno and then Amalfi with its relics of Andrew. He saw the reputed tomb of Virgil and all the places in the neighbourhood that held associations with the Classical era or which preserved actual relics of antiquity.

In 1458, Aeneas Silvius Piccolomini was elected Pope Pius II. Within two years the Turks, under Sultan Mehemet II, had invaded the Greek

Peloponnesus. Anxious to preserve his own skin, Thomas Palaeologus, the despot of Morea and brother to the last Christian emperor of Constantinople, seized what was said to be the head of the Apostle Andrew from Patras and took it, together with his family, to Corfu, hoping to use the relic as a bargaining counter for ensuring his safety.

The pope, on hearing that Palaeolologus was likely to sell the head to the highest bidder, wrote to Thomas asking him to bring it to Rome, to be placed beside the bones of Andrew's brother St Peter. Pius promised to shelter both the head and the Despot as long as danger threatened, in the possibility that Thomas (and the head) might one day be restored.

Thomas Palaeologus landed at Ancona on the north-east coast of Italy on 16 Nov 1460 but did not arrive in Rome till 7 March of the following year. The head of St Andrew, meanwhile, was deposited in the citadel of Narni until the pope could regain control over the civil unrest in and around Rome.

Finally, with his wife and four children, Palaeologus arrived in Rome during Lent of 1461. Pius was full of sympathy for the exile and gave him lodgings at San Spirito in Sassia (where Pius would later also deposit other relics of the Apostle Andrew).

When peace was finally restored, Pius sent out proclamations to the chief cities of Italy promising indulgences, saying that the more people who were present in Rome, the more magnificent the head's welcome would be.

Pius had planned to bring out the heads of the Apostles Peter and Paul to greet the head of St Andrew, but they were so weighed down with lead and silver that they had to be left on view at the Lateran.

The approach to the basilica of St Peter were quickly upgraded to cope with the crowds who were to come to be inspired with belief in the eventual triumph of the Christians over the Turks. New steps were constructed and two colossal statues of Saints Peter and Paul by Paolo Romano were erected on each side at the base of the steps.

The ceremony of St Andrew's head took place during Easter week 1462. Whole houses had been cleared from the piazza of St Peter's and, inside the church, the tombs of medieval popes and cardinals in the middle of the nave were pushed to the sides of the building.

Near the Ponte Molle (the Milvian Bridge), to commemorate the ceremony of St Andrew's head, a marble tabernacle (tent-shaped box) was erected on the spot where Pius would receive the relic along with a statue of St Andrew, again by Paolo Romano, so confirming the symbolic link with Constantine.

Inside the basilica itself, a chapel was dedicated to St Andrew. It contained a tabernacle supporting a ceremonial cup, with gilded marble reliefs of the Apostle's head by Paolo Romano and Isaia da Pisa. Inside, was the silver-gilt reliquary by Simone da Firenze. For the occasion the platform from which Pius showed the Apostle's head to the assembled crowds was hung with tapestries. It was probably later dismantled afterwards, as the pope left Rome in May 1462 and did not come back until December.

Six weeks before the ceremony, Pius had called together his six most trusted cardinals and confided in them his deep concern about the Turkish successes which were threatening to overwhelm Christianity in the Levant. Pius was making an effort to win the support of the self-interested princes for a Crusade through the startling public relations coup offered by the ceremony of St Andrew's head. He planned to use the event to ask St Andrew's help through St Peter and St Paul so that, by defeating the Turks it would be possible for the head to return in glory to Greece, and for Thomas Palaeologus to return to power.

The Milvian Bridge (Ponte Milvio/Ponte Molle) over the River Tiber. (Courtesy Br John Hugh Parker)

Close to the Milvian Bridge, on the first day of the ceremony, Palm Sunday, 12 April 1462, Pius, very moved, received the head from a weeping Cardinal Basilios Bessarion (a Greek expatriate scholar and theologian, cardinal from 1439-72 and titular Latin patriarch of Constantinople). A pen and ink drawing attributed to Ventura Salimbeni, now in the Museo Horne in Florence, records the occasion.

After Pius' speech of welcome – and a short prayer that by the Apostle's intercession, the insolence of the faithless Turk might be crushed – the choir sang a hymn. That night the head remained at the church of Santa Maria del Popolo. The superstitious Romans were restive as there was a storm during the night. However, the next day was radiant and filled then crowds with anticipation of a magnificent ceremony.

St Peter's, Rome. (Author's copyright)

The front of the two-mile procession through the centre of Rome reached St Peter's before the pope – carried in his golden chair and holding St Andrew's head sheltered from the sun by a golden canopy – could start from Santa Maria del Popolo. St Peter's was already filled with a crowd of strangers and from them arose a great noise of voices like the murmur of many waters, and at the sight of the Apostle's head 'all fell to beating their breasts and with groans and wailings commended themselves to it'.

Although it can be assumed that some Scots were present – such as members of the papal administration – Piccolomini, in his description of the foreign dignitaries present, does not mention any from Scotland. Inside the basilica it seemed one blaze of lights and there was the glow of innumerable lamps and candelabra, made still more marvellous by the music of the organ and the singing of the clergy.

The head of St Andrew was set down on the altar and Cardinal Bessarion, on behalf of St Andrew, addressed St Peter and then the pope, urging him not to stop exhorting Christian princes to support the Crusade through which one day they would win everlasting fame.

It was the supreme moment of Piccolomini's life.

On Easter Sunday, the head was exhibited along with the veil of Veronica, the Volto Santo. At the end of the ceremonies, the head was deposited in the Castel' Sant' Angelo until a proper receptacle could be prepared for it. This was not done until the following year, when not only was a new reliquary made, but also a tent-shaped box on four supporting columns.

Pius, in a gesture commemorating Gregory the Great's acquisition of the relic of St Andrew in Constantinople, placed the reliquary over Gregory's tomb, which he had moved to a new chapel in the course of reorganising the basilica. The statue of St Andrew which later stood on St Gregory's tomb was placed there in 1570 by Pius' descendant, Francesco Bandini Piccolomini.

The white and gilded marble cup could not be missed by those who entered the church. Three marble reliefs by Isaia da Pisa and Paolo Romano (from the lunettes of the cup) survive today in the Grotte Vaticane. The original Patras reliquary was later sent to Pienza after the new one (77cm/30in high) was made.

At a secret consistory on 23 Sept 1463, following the reception of St Andrew's head, the pope urged the Church to return to abstinence, purity, innocence, zeal for the faith, religious fervour, scorn of death and eagerness of martyrdom in preparation for the Crusade on which he would set out on 18 June 1464. 'We must', urged Pius II, 'draw near to those earlier saints'.

The significance of the St Andrew chapel in the history of St Peter's is considerable. It could be said that it was the first time a Renaissance pope had cleared a prominent place in the basilica not only for a specific saint, but for himself. Pius ordered that he should be buried in the chapel, thus once more identifying his heartfelt cause with that of St Andrew – the proposed Crusade against the Turks which was to lead to Pius' eventual disappointment and death. Pius' lengthy description of the complex ceremonies offer some suggestion as to the spirit in which the Great Morbrac, with its reliquary of the Apostle, was celebrated at St Andrews.

As for the Piccolomini family, it continued to forge strong personal links with the major locations of the bones of St Andrew. Aeneas Sylvius' nephew Antonio was created Duke of Amalfi around 1463, while Alexander Piccolomini (later Pius III) was consecrated Archbishop of Patras a century later. In the time of Pius V, St Andrew's chapel in St Peter's was demolished and Pius's tomb transferred to the church of Sant' Andrea della Valle.

Nine years later there were fresh ecclesiastical developments in Scotland. When Patrick Graham became its first archbishop in 1472, the see of St Andrews was elevated to the dignity of an archbishopric with metropolitan status. The bull of Pope Sixtus IV (1414-84), elevated Bishop Graham to the rank of Archbishop and made all 12 Scottish bishops suffragans under the see of St Andrews.

Hitherto, the Archbishops of York had tried to extend their jurisdiction over the Scottish bishoprics (especially over Galloway), while the bishoprics of the Isles and of Orkney had been subject to the see of Trondheim in Norway. An important Papal decision was emphasised by the reissue of a bull of Clement III ordering that papal judges delegate were to hear Scottish cases in Scotland or Durham or Carlisle but never in York.

By their patronage of the shrine at St Andrews, the monarchs of Scotland and England confirmed the status of St Andrews Cathedral and its relics. King Edward I and his queen came there in 1300 and each presented a golden *ouch* (bracelet) to adorn the relics of the Apostle.

In March 1303, only four years before his death, Edward I and his second wife, Queen Margaret (sister of Philip IV of France), came to the town, each offering a jewelled gold buckle at the priory church to decorate the arm of St Andrew. The queen's gift, made on 19 March, was valued at seven merks. On the same day, she gave an ornament of gold to the same value at the shrine of St Margaret at Dunfermline. Four days later, the king followed his wife by presenting a similar gift (valued at six merks) for the relics of St Andrew.

St Andrew's Day was a time for rejoicing as well as thanksgiving, popular with the kings and queens of Scotland. In 1461 the pious Queen Mary of Gueldres, probably influenced by Burgundian piety, visited the shrine of St Andrew. The urbane and highly civilised King James IV made frequent offerings there throughout his reign. The poet and herald Sir David Lindsay wrote that the king celebrated St Andrew's Day with great ceremony:

> *And ilk year for his Patron's saik,*
> *Ane banquet royall wald he maik,*
> *With wylde fowle, venisoun and wyne,*
> *With tairt and falm and fruitage fyne;*
> *Of bran and geill[25] there was na skant,*
> *And ypooras[26] he wald not want.*

King James V and Marie de Lorraine were married in the cathedral in

June 1538 and it was in St Andrews that, a year later, the king's eldest son, James Stewart, was born.

There is a question over the relative importance of the Scottish shrines. To some extent, there was a fashion in saints and pilgrimage. The 'four heid pilgrimages' of Scotland, in their order of importance during the reign of James IV, have been identified as St Ninian's *Candida Casa* (Whithorn in Dumfries and Galloway), St Duthac's shrine in Tain, Ross-shire, Our Lady of the Hamer at Whitekirk, East Lothian and the tomb of St Adrian on the Isle of May in the River Forth. During the reign of James V, there were apparently only three 'heid pilgrimages' – Whithorn, Tain and St Andrews.

The only surviving record of pilgrim numbers is a figure of 15,653 who came to Whitekirk in 1413. This figure is recorded in a document in the Vatican Library, a copy of which was brought back from Rome by Sir David Baird of Newbyth. One can only guess at the numbers who came to St Andrews.

In a letter to Pope Innocent X, James IV assures him that pilgrims from England, Ireland and the adjoining countries yearly flocked to Whithorn. Accordingly, a charter of James IV underlines the need to provide the bodily wants of pilgrims at Whithorn.

Although many pilgrims were genuine, the role of pilgrim provided an ideal 'cover' for those with nefarious intent. Only a few years before the Scottish Reformation (1560), international art dealers were already planning to pillage the cultural wealth of the weakened Roman Catholic administration in Scotland. In 1553 Marcus Wagner, an agent of the Lutheran theologian, Matthias Flacius Illyricus, was able to gain access to the priory at St Andrews posing as a Catholic pilgrim calling on his way to Jerusalem.

With considerable subterfuge he managed to remove a number of rare volumes which are today preserved in the Herzog August Library at Wolfenbüttel, Germany, having escaped the fate of the rest of the priory's collection. The stolen manuscript was compiled in the 13th century and contains a substantial proportion of music written specifically for St Andrews.

For the well-to-do, as Chaucer's *Canterbury Tales* reminds us, the journey to a shrine could be a flamboyant and entertaining affair. When in October 1504, King James set out on pilgrimage to Tain, he did so accompanied by dogs and hawks and enjoyed sport on the way. He was entertained by four Italian minstrels; young girls performed dances and pipe-organs were carried in his retinue to be used at the divine service. Two years later, in very different circumstances – James made the journey from Edinburgh to Whithorn, apparently on foot, to pray for the queen's recovery from childbirth.

There are at least two known cases where penitents were ordered to have recourse to the 'heid pilgrimages'. This they could do in person, or by proxy – by giving a stipend to a priest to celebrate mass on their behalf. This was also one of the ways of providing a modest income for ordinary clerics.

John White of Edinburgh, in expiation of the crime of murder, agreed in May 1525 to pay the father of his victim 100 marks, and to pay a priest to celebrate requiem masses at Scala Celi in Rome and at the four 'heid pilgrimages' of Scotland.[27] Five years later the feuding Kerrs and the Scotts were to seek forgiveness by going to the four 'heid pilgrimages' of Scotland to arrange for masses to be celebrated for the soul of Andrew Ker of Cesford and those killed with him in the field at Melrose.

9

St Andrews Cathedral and The Reformation

THE CATHEDRAL OF ST ANDREWS was the scene of many historic events. On 3 February 1414, for example, all the church bells rang to welcome the bulls of foundation for the privileges of the new University of St Andrews. They had been granted by the elderly pope, Benedict XIII, in his fortress-retreat of Peñiscola in Aragon, Spain.

After the bulls had been formally presented to Bishop Henry Wardlaw in the Augustinian priory, the diocesan clergy and the canons processed to the high altar of the cathedral, reaching it just before the 10am mass was due to begin. That day was spent in continuous rejoicing and, at night, the streets of the town were lit up by bonfires.

Over a century later, in 1538, the French princess, Marie de Lorraine, celebrated her wedding to James V at the cathedral with mass, singing and the playing of the organ. Afterwards the king and Queen dined in the abbey accompanied by *shawms* (a tenor oboe), trumpets and other instruments. The Lord Lyon, Sir David Lindsay of the Mount, presented pageants which were interspersed with feasting and jousting.

It seems to have become customary to baptise princes of Scotland at St Andrews. In 1264, Alexander, son of King Alexander III, was christened by Gamelin, bishop of St Andrews. Although the future James III was born in Stirling, it was not until two years later that he was baptised at St Andrews and his princely style proclaimed. Conversely, the king's eldest son was baptised at St Andrews in 1539 and named James Stewart, Duke of Rothesay and Prince of Scotland. By the beginning of the 16th century, however, St Andrews had declined as a pilgrimage centre. The 1518 charter of St Leonard's College notes that:

> ... the wonders for which the relics became famous brought so many pilgrims from diverse lands that a hospital (hostel) was built, but as the pilgrimages and miracles had in a measure ceased, so that the hospital was without pilgrims.

The hospital was now to be converted into a college, along with St Leonard's church. The writer adds that the miracles at St Andrews had ceased because, in course of time, the Christian faith had established itself in Scotland – there was no longer any need for miracles to convert unbelievers or waverers.

The distinction between pilgrim and tourist was hard to see. Pilgrims were tourists, moving with little hindrance through international borders. As previously mentioned this is well illustrated by the ease with which the professional manuscript-procurer, Marcus Wagner, an agent for the Lutheran scholar and theologian Matthias Flacius Illyricus, gained access to the Augustinian priory in 1553. Illyricus directed an operation across Europe to collect Roman Catholic manuscripts by fair means or foul, in order to use as evidence of corruption in the history of the Church that he was compiling. Wagner posed as a pilgrim who was visiting St Andrews on his way to Jerusalem and easily managed to remove some of the Augustinians' most precious volumes, including the St Andrews Music Book which is today fortunately in the safety of the Herzog August Bibliothek in Wolfenbüttel.

Heresy Trials and Assassination

But it was the heresy trials and executions staged at St Andrews Cathedral that would haunt the memory of the Reformers, as much as its role as a centre of administration or the wealth that the church contained.

On 23 July 1433, probably after a trial in the cathedral, Paul Kravar, a Wyclifite theologian and paramedic from Prague, was burned publicly at St Andrews. Patrick Hamilton, an academic and composer, was tried for his Lutheran beliefs in the church and sentenced to be burned at the stake as a heretic on 29 February 1527. His trial was presided over by Archbishop James Beaton and his nephew David (later, Cardinal) Beaton. Then the Benedictine monk Henry Forrest, after a trial in the cathedral, was burned at the north church style so that all the people of Forfar would see the fire and be frightened from taking up the same Reformed doctrine.

Heresy trials were staged with deliberate formality. There would be tiers of seats for the dignitaries, erected against the chancel-screen. This intimidating phalanx rose above the platform where the prosecutor stood, dressed in a white surplice with a blood-red hood hanging down his back. The accused was placed on another platform and the rest of the church was crammed with the devout and the curious standing to watch the drama unfold.

The Reformer George Wishart was tried in 1546 at the cathedral in front of Cardinal David Beaton. Proceedings began with John Winram, sub-prior of St Andrews, preaching from the prosecutor's platform on the parable of the Wheat and the Cockle – the final separation and burning of alien and noxious growths. This was only a prelude to Wishart's death by fire on 1 March 1546. Wishart's execution persuaded many of the young novices in the Abbey, led by John Winram himself, to lean towards the Protestant faith.

Three months later, however, on 29 May 1546, Cardinal David Beaton, Archbishop of St Andrews and Chancellor of Scotland, was murdered by the Reformers in his palace at St Andrews. Twelve years later, on 20 April 1558, John Winram was again amongst the bishops and abbots at the final heresy trial held in the cathedral, that of the last Protestant martyr, Walter Myln, parish priest of Lunan, then over 80 years of age.

Destruction of the Cathedral

Just over a year later, on Sunday 11 June 1559, John Knox entered St Andrews and preached in the parish church on the ejection by Jesus of the buyers and sellers from the Temple. Knox preached for the next three days. Then on Wednesday 14 June 1559 the work of destruction began:

> .... they fell to purge the kirk and break down the altars and images and all kind of idolatrie ... and before the sun wes down there was never inch standing but bare walls. Bot the idols that were in the Abbay were brought to the north of the said Abbay ... and there they burned the whole idols.

In a fitting irony, the statues of the saints from the cathedral church were publicly burned on the very spot where Walter Myln had been cruelly executed by fire in April 1558.

This was a well-organised plan to destroy altars, images of saints, vestments, liturgical books and other equipment of the traditional liturgy – referred to as the 'monuments of idolatrie'. The furnishings of the cathedral were broken and burnt. Nothing survived to show the quality of woodcarving or painting, manuscript illumination, stained glass or embroidery. Only a fine 13th-century head of Christ and fragments of Bishop Wardlaw's tomb remained. Four centuries of liturgical worship came to an abrupt end.

St Andrews Cathedral and St Rule's Tower. (Author's copyright)

All items of precious metals were taken away – bell-metal, brass plaques, lead, timber, slates and other building material would be removed by the prior, James Stewart, who would be assassinated at Linlithgow in 1570. On 6 January 1561, the silver-work, brass, ceremonial vestments and ornaments of the parish church were sold by public auction.

The late, eminent medieval historian Professor Geoffrey Barrow commented:

> In its day St Andrews was as famous as St Thomas and Canterbury. I think probably you could say it was one of the most important half-dozen, or even three or four, in Northern Europe. I think it was wiped out at the Reformation. There is very little literature on this. There was a reluctance in the 18th and 19th centuries to take any of these things seriously because the ethos in Scotland was so strongly Protestant and Presbyterian.[28]

The revenues of the priory were siphoned off to the king until the death of James V, after which they seem to have gone to the young prior's mother, Margaret Douglas, at Loch Leven, today within the boundary of Perth and Kinross Council.

However, in Scotland the change from Roman Catholic to Reformed was not a dramatic one but more of a gradual process. The case of the population of St Andrews, which went to bed one evening as Roman Catholics and awoke the next morning to find themselves Protestants, was not typical.

The Scottish Reformation obliterated almost all of the evidence for the nature of popular devotion in Scotland. Today, such evidence is much harder to find than in England where church furnishings and monuments had been less thoroughly and systematically eradicated than in Scotland. However, it should be remembered that the Reformers, while stripping out the furnishings of churches, were careful to preserve the fabric of the buildings to be re-furbished as Reformed kirks. No substantial damage was done to the essential fabric of St Andrews Cathedral, for example, at the time of the Reformation.

In terms of human lives, the Scottish Reformation was much less violent than that in England, where some 300 Protestants were executed under Queen Mary Tudor (1553-8) and around 156 Catholics under Queen Elizabeth I (1558-1603). In Scotland 21 Protestants were executed before 1559 and three Catholic priests.

Yet, no matter how 'velvet' a revolution it was, the systematic eradication of Roman and papal theological and liturgical traditions took place all over Scotland. At Glasgow Cathedral images, paintings, glass and other 'relicks of popery' were destroyed. Only a few of the cathedral's treasures were spirited abroad by James Beaton, the last of the medieval archbishops. So complete was the expunging of the visible signs of the Roman rite that the only pre-Reformation image of St Mungo still to be seen today is in Germany, at Cologne Cathedral.[29]

On 29 June 1559 the army of the Lords of the Congregation entered Edinburgh. St Giles was pillaged and its altars destroyed. Jewels, silver vessels and vestments were sold by order of the magistrates and the proceeds used to pay for repairs to the fabric of the church. From that time the church was renamed the High Kirk of Edinburgh.

Some time after the Reformation the relic of St Giles – whose wooden statue had been previously burnt and sunk into the Nor' Loch – was taken out of its silver reliquary and deposited in the safe-keeping of the Dean of Guild. The diamond from the ring on its finger was sold and the arm bone buried in St Giles kirkyard.

Destruction continued sporadically over the following years. At Holyroodhouse, six service-books of the Chapel Royal were burnt in 1569 by order of the Regent Moray. Four years later, the Regent Morton burned all the vestments and liturgical books of the town of Haddington in East Lothian.

John Winram and the Relics of St Andrew

Two of the key players in the disposal of the treasures of St Andrews Cathedral were Alexander Stewart, Prior of the Augustinian canons (one of the illegitimate sons of James V) and his sub-prior, John Winram.

St Giles (Daniel Wilson, *Memorials of Old Edinburgh*, 1868). In 1829 the exterior of the building was encased in a skin of smooth ashlar by the architect William Burn.

In 1544, as part of his 'Rough Wooing', Henry VIII ordered the destruction of the Bishop's Palace in St Andrews and of the cathedral. Stewart and Winram were instructed by Cardinal Beaton to remove the entire treasures of the cathedral and palace to the safety of Portmoak Priory by the shores of Loch Leven. Even though some of the cathedral treasures were held in custodianship for the Scottish people, they were *de facto* the property of the Church authorities and it was the Cardinal's responsibility to ensure their safety.

Three of the chests contained relics and silk and gold cloths with other liturgical items belonging to St Andrews which the canons placed for safety at Loch Leven. Apparently nothing was lost during this exercise. Everything that was taken to Portmoak Priory was safely returned to St Andrews.

This was probably the first time in two centuries that the entire contents of the cathedral, including the Great Morbrac, was moved to safety – which meant that Stewart, but Windram in particular, had the responsibility of overseeing the transfer. They would draw up the inventory. These two people knew the entire contents of the cathedral and the Bishop's Palace at first hand. They had practical experience of identifying, handling and packaging every artefact in the cathedral treasure. In the event, everything was safely brought back when the danger passed for, instead of destroying the Bishop's Palace, Henry VIII's forces wrecked Dundee.

The exiled Roman Catholic historian and Benedictine Abbot Ninian Winzet (1518-92), observed that John Winram was neither a good Catholic nor a good Protestant, but a damned good heathen. The illustrator Jurek Pütter comments:

> Winram was one of history's great snakes in the grass. He was the type of great opportunist who, for example, had the Reformation not been successful, would have been one of the first to strut back onto the stage of history as the saviour of the relics of Andrew the Apostle.
>
> Winram, a man who had devoted himself to chastity, charity and poverty, died an exceedingly wealthy man. At his death, his sizeable family argued over his fortune, which was valued (in present-day money) at between seven and nine million pounds. His gravestone still exists, much mutilated, at St Leonard's church in St Leonard's College.
>
> The finger of suspicion points back to these two individuals who had a very intimate knowledge and who managed the transportation of all of the relics – Alexander Stewart and John Winram. They were the two principal figures, when the Reformed religion consolidated itself, who were in material terms the absolute winners.
>
> There is something to suggest that Winram, perhaps, removed the relics of Andrew the Apostle and so there is a strong possibility that a supreme manipulator like Winram would have had the relics built into a piece of furniture. This was a strategy often used in the later Middle Ages to safeguard great treasures. After Winram's death, there would be no need for the relics to be restored. In time the relics in the furniture may have been dispersed or destroyed.
>
> The Great Morbrac, the so-called twelve houses, (the house within a house within a house), was disposed of by Stewart and Winram. They effectively cut it up. Something of their fabulous wealth can be attributed to the cutting-up, the melting-down, the disposal of the gold, the silver, the precious and semi-precious stones.

Pütter argues that:

> It is a possibility that the relic in its hiding-place passed
> into the possession of his family and even survives today
> unrecognised in a kist (wooden chest) or a dresser with
> a secret compartment. I do believe that the relics of St
> Andrew still exist. My hunch tells me that they still exist,
> not recognised or seen for what they really are. Stewart
> and Winram are the safest bets. They are highly unpleas-
> ant individuals and that makes them more interesting
> because their motives are much more discernible but
> transparent because of their duplicity.

Nevertheless, in spite of the best efforts of the Reformers to stamp out
what they regarded as idolatrous superstitions, the urge to go on pilgrimage took some time to die. An Act of the Scottish Parliament of
1581 speaks of 'the perverse inclination to superstition through
which the dregs of idolatry still remain in various parts of the realm
by using pilgrimages to certain chapels, wells, crosses and other monuments of idolatry, as well as observing festival days of the saints,
sometimes building bonfires or singing carols inside or around kirks'.

A Statute of 1593 makes it clear that travelling beggars were even
more indistinguishable from pilgrims. Vagabonds and strong beggars
pretending they were passing in pilgrimage to chapels and wells had
become a recognised public nuisance. However, pilgrimage persisted
stubbornly, even to such an unlikely spot as Peebles in the Borders,
where the Holy Cross continued to be an object of veneration as it
had been for James IV who had embellished the cross with precious
metals.

An ordinance as late as 1599 was given to the minister of
Innerleithen in the Borders, Mr William Sanderson and some of the
brethren, to await with certain gentlemen and bailies of Peebles to
apprehend those who came in pilgrimage to the Cross Kirk. The band
of vigilantes was duly successful in catching a number of local men
and women who had come to pray in the old way.

Even two years later, it was necessary to take steps once more to
turn pilgrims away. Persons who superstitiously went to the Cross
Kirk at Beltane were to be apprehended and punished by the magistrates.

10
Images of St Andrew

Patron of Scotland
The historian and Reformer George Buchanan records that St
Andrew was looked upon as the patron saint of Scotland during the
reign of Malcolm Canmore (1057-93). It is very likely that, from King
Malcolm's reign, St Andrew's Day would be widely celebrated as a
national festival. Events of national importance were held on 30
November quite deliberately – the coronation of John Balliol, for
example, in 1292. After Balliol had been deposed, an English song told
Scots to go to the Devil as St Andrew could no longer protect them!

From the early medieval period, St Andrew was the saint most likely
to be called upon in time of war. In 1173 King William the Lion swore
by St Andrew that he would stay in England and fight for his hereditary
rights in Northumberland. There is little doubt that from that time, at
least, 'Saint Andrew' was one of the principal battle cries of the Scots.

According to the poet Blind Harry (1470-92) in his *Acts and Deeds
of Sir William Wallace*, the prayer of the patriot William Wallace (1274-
1305) was: 'Saint Andrew mot us speed' ('Saint Andrew will give us
success'). In 1303 before the Triple Battle of Roslin in Midlothian, Sir
Simon Fraser addressed the Scottish leaders with the words: 'In God
all your hope ye set; Saint Andrew, Saint Ninian and Saint Margaret'.

At the Battle of Bannockburn 11 years later, the Scottish soldiers
had the white cross of St
Andrew on their tunics. Before
battle began they knelt in
prayer, invoking the protection
of their patron saint.

Monument to the Triple Battle of Roslin, 24 Feb
1303. (Author's copyright)

This growing national consensus was given fuller public
recognition when, four years
later, King Robert the Bruce, at
the dedication of St Andrews
Cathedral on 5 July 1318, laid a
parchment on the High Altar

expressing the nation's thanks for the victory at Bannockburn.

It is the Declaration of Arbroath of 1320 which most urgently and completely asserts the integrity of the Scottish nation and its right to exist, free from the threats of subjugation so frequently issued by its predatory southern neighbour.[30] Framed during a Scottish Parliament at Arbroath, in which the king and the Three Estates (clergy, nobility and burgesses) were present, the Declaration gathered together what the Scots believed to be unassailable evidence and water-tight arguments for Scotland's right to papal protection from the persistent territorial ambitions and incursions of the English throne.

Cleverly, the Declaration did so by first stressing the familial bonds between Scotland and the person of Pope John XXII ('Most holy father ... your obedient and devoted sons ... '). There followed a stern reminder to Rome of the genealogy of the Scottish nation. By ancient tradition, the ancestors of the Scots were Scythians from southern Russia who had later emigrated northwards to Scotland, first across the Mediterranean and then from the Atlantic seaboard of Spain.

While still in Scythia, it was the ancestors of the Scots, the Declaration records, who were one of the earliest peoples to be evangelised by the first Apostle, Andrew. This claim to be the legitimate 'first-born' followers of Christ asserted the Scots' right to be treated with positive discrimination by the papacy.

Equally, the leaders of the Scottish nation reinforced its claim by also citing the ties of blood which bound the successor of Peter to the forefathers of the Scots living on the shores of the Black Sea. During his missionary labours, Peter's brother Andrew had bestowed his personal patronage on the Scythians for all time.

Oppressed by the English king's looting and the massacre of Scottish religious communities and his cruel treatment of the Scottish people in general – the Scots bishops, the nobility and burgesses saw in King Robert I the inheritor of the leadership qualities shown by biblical fighters for freedom such as Maccabeus and Joshua. In investing their leader with this legendary heroism the Scots, fresh from the triumph of Bannockburn, pointed to indisputable evidence of divine support for their ventures, just as Eusebius had done for Constantine and Fordun and Bower did for King Angus. Historically, Maccabeus had taken command of the Jewish patriots in 166 BC, had driven the enemy out, purified the Temple and restored the ancient worship of Jehovah. Similarly, Joshua succeeded Moses as leader of the Israelites. After 40 years of wandering through the desert the people of Israel were led by him to the promised land.

In a later Scottish medieval context such comparisons imply that the centre of Scotland's military and religious power and its search for freedom were now focused through leaders such as Bruce and Wallace but also through the national church, the Cathedral at St Andrews. In their letter to the pope the Scots then go on to suggest that conflicts between Christian nations would damage the stability of the papacy and affect its credibility. Finally, they appeal to a cause dear to the pope's heart – the crusade. If Rome forces Edward to stop his incursions into Scotland, then both Scotland and England would be free to send men on the Crusade to liberate the Holy Places. Thus, the Declaration of Arbroath was skilfully presented to appeal to the Roman administration and was central to establishing Scotland's historical rights to a separate national identity and an indigenous culture.

Even after the Reformation, St Andrew continued to have a place of honour in the Scottish psyche. Andrew Melville (1545-1622), one of the leaders of the Scottish Reformation, had a strong regard for Scotland's patron saint, writing:

> Saint Andrew, Christ's Apostle true
> Does sign the Scotsmen's rites;
> Saint George, Armenian heresiarch,
> The Englishmen delights.
> Let Scotsmen then hold fast the Faith
> That is wholly apostolic,
> Howbeit that England keeps the course
> That is wholly apostatic.

Here, Melville is alluding to the fact that during the Western Schism (1378 to 1418) Scotland stayed loyal to the Pope in Avignon, while England supported the anti-pope in Rome. Centuries later, the discrepancy between Saint George and Saint Andrew which so delighted Melville was diplomatically resolved on 15 March 1603 when King James VI and I, Queen Anne and Prince Henry solemnly processed from the Tower of London to Whitehall. There had, according to the entertainment scripted by the playwright Thomas Dekker (1570-1632), been great apprehension that the country would be torn apart by civil war after the death of Queen Elizabeth I.

But the 'feared wounds of a civil sword' were prevented from bursting forth by the sound of the trumpets that proclaimed James as king. 'All eyes,' wrote Dekker, 'were presently turned north to behold this 45 years' wonder now brought forth by time.'

What the king and his new subjects in London saw was Dekker's extraordinary allegorical pageant. From opposite sides of the street appeared two knights on horseback and in full armour, draped with the heraldic arms of England and Scotland.

Anachronistically, England's patron, Saint George, symbolically met the fisherman Andrew – now also dressed in shining armour. The two saints grasped hands before the expectant crowds to 'testify their leagued combination and new sworn brotherhood' and so, as they rode towards the king, both saints promoted the hoped-for political unity of the new Britain.

Freemasons in Scotland

St Andrew not only figured in times of war or political struggle. His patronage was claimed by ordinary working people. In medieval times the association of incorporated trades grew out of the need to protect its craftsmen and tradesmen from exploitation by merchants or town councils. In Scotland working stonemasons formed themselves into incorporations. King James I sometimes visited and supported their 'lodges', on one occasion paying a revenue of £4 Scots to every master mason, and to a grand master whose office was to regulate the fraternity.

Scottish stonemasons' lodges, built where prolonged building activities were taking place, are recorded at Aberdeen and Dundee in the late 15th and early 16th century. However, these seem to have been dissolved around the time of the Scottish Reformation (1560). By 1475, the masons and wrights (carpenters) of Edinburgh had enough collective power to be able to agree a 'seal of cause' (charter) from the city of Edinburgh allowing them to act as an incorporation, an early form of guild which set out the craft regulations. In 1489 coopers and other tradesmen joined the incorporation, whose function was to rule on disputes, supply charity to its members and also control apprenticeships and the entrance to the trades.

Although most trades had such incorporations, the stonemasons had a unique feature in the lodge. In 1491 the Edinburgh burgh authorities gave the stonemasons the right to have recreation in their common lodge, suggesting that the lodge was more than a place for storing tools but also had a social and recreational function.

In 1583 King James VI appointed William Schaw as master of the work and warden general, with a commission to re-organise the stonemasons' craft. Accordingly, in 1598 he issued the Schaw Statutes setting out the rights and obligations of the stonemasons. Penalties were to be imposed for poor workmanship or any breaches of safety codes. A second Statute was drawn up by Schaw in 1599 which referred to esoteric knowledge and confirmed the fact that the mother lodge of Scotland, Lodge Mother Kilwinning No 0 was already in existence. Schaw instructed all lodges to keep written records, fix the times of regular meetings, test members on their knowledge of the craft and record the attendance and progress of apprentices. For this reason William Schaw is looked upon as the founding father of modern Freemasonry.

In the 16th and 17th centuries men of importance were admitted to the Scottish lodges, even if they were not tradesmen and so, gradually, the membership changed in nature. Among the first non-stonemasons to join a Scottish lodge in 1598 were William Schaw himself and James Boswell of Auchinleck. In 1634 William Lord Alexander, his brother Lord Anthony and Sir Alexander Strachen of Thornton were initiated into the Lodge of Edinburgh (St Mary's Chapel) No 1.

Many aspects of medieval masonry would later be adopted by modern Freemasonry: these included the craft history, the connection between masonry and mathematics – including secret signs and words and initiation rituals (originally used to protect standards of craft workmanship).

Grand Master's Jewel. (Robert LD Cooper by courtesy of the Grand Lodge of Scotland)

From Schaw's time to the early 18th-century masonry changed to an organisation led not by craftsmen but by men who were not trained in working stone. In 1717 there were Scottish lodges in Edinburgh, Kilwinning, Inverness, Dundee, Stirling, Aberdeen and Glasgow. On 30 November 1736 representatives from 33 lodges met in Edinburgh. The Grand Lodge was formed and William St Clair of Roslin was elected the first grand master mason. Hence, St Andrew and his saltire cross featured prominently in Masonic regalia.

Freemasons of note included the Lord Provost of Edinburgh, George Drummond (grand master mason of Scotland 1752-3), the architect Robert Adam (1728-92), the poet Robert

Burns (1759-96), the novelist Sir Walter Scott (1771-1832) and, in the 20th century, King George VI (1895-1952) and the entertainer Sir Harry Lauder (1870-1950). Today there are some 665 active lodges in Scotland and 499 overseas, with a world membership of around six million.

The first St Andrew's Society

St Andrew was also often adopted as the patron of groups devoted to argument and scholarly discussion. In the National Library of Scotland is a small notebook which records the activities of a St Andrew's Society which flourished at Edinburgh University between 1765 and 1767.[31]

Proceedings began on 9 Jan 1765 with a Mr Balfour presiding. Members met to listen to Mr Andrew Scot deliver 'a Discourse upon the Causes of that Propensity in man to credit a Person's Representation of himself.' The question debated was whether the study of history or poetry was most valuable. Later that year members met in Dr Young's Schools to tease out the problem of whether men were happier as savages or as civilised and whether women should be allowed to study literature! In the following year members were asked to discuss whether the toleration of different religious opinion was consistent with the interests of civil society. Among new members in 1768 was the Whig advocate Henry Erskine, later to become Lord Advocate.

As well as being invoked by intellectuals and the well-to-do, St Andrew was used by the working class as a symbol for asserting national status and financial solidarity and security: The St Andrew Order of Ancient Free Gardeners' Friendly Society, for example. In the National Library of Scotland is the register of The City of Edinburgh Lodge No 1 Branch. The first entry is dated 17 December 1887 and lists, among others, a cooper (aged 43), a bootmaker (33), a warehouseman (43) and a plumber (29). The last entry of 3 September 1929, ends with the name of a gasfitter (aged 45).[32]

Sir Walter Scott

Even that staunch supporter of the Treaty of Union, Sir Walter Scott, saw the unifying potential in St Andrew of Scotland. On 14 August 1822 Scott welcomed King George IV to the Port of Leith, to the north of Edinburgh:

Sir Walter Scott was admitted on board the royal yacht

and was graciously received by the King. The object was
to present a St Andrew's cross to His Majesty, in the
name of a party of distinguished ladies in Edinburgh.
The Sisters of the Silver Cross. This cross was formed of
pearls on blue velvet with a belt of gold, on which was
embroidered with pearls the following Gaelic motto,
Riagh Albaim gu brath! – Hail to the King of Scotland!
This elegant and costly emblem of Scotland was the
work of Mrs Skene of Rubislaw, the sister of Sir William
Forbes. It was graciously received by His Majesty and
worn in his hat during his stay in Scotland.

Russia

In Russia, the legend of their patron St Andrew's preaching journeys
continued to have great potency. The Russians and the Greeks maintained an uneasy relationship at the time of the Byzantine Empire. In
the year AD 988 the Emperor Basil II asked the Russian Prince
Vladimir (AD 956-1015) for help. The Prince dispatched an army of
6,000 Russian mercenaries who arrived in Constantinople and managed to save the emperor's throne. In the same year a mass baptism of
Kievans took place in the waters of the River Dnieper.

From AD 1039, strong religious links between the Russians and
Constantinople were forged which were only broken when, in 1448,
the Russian bishops severed their dependence on the Unionist pri-
mate of Constantinople and elected their own primate, making the
Russian Church a metropolitan diocese of the Byzantine Patriarchate.
Vladimir I's grandson, Vsevolod, founded the first Russian church
dedicated to St Andrew, and also had his own son, Vladimir
Monomakh take the baptismal name of Andrew. A grandson of
Vsevolod (Andrey Dobryy died 1142) and a great-grandson (Andrey
Bogolyubskiy died 1174) were the first Russian princes to be known
by the name of Andrew.

As late as the 16th century the St Andrew legend still persisted. In
1582, when Ivan the Terrible met the papal envoy Antonio Possevino
in Moscow, he boasted that the Russians had received their Christian
faith from St Andrew the Apostle on the shores of the Black Sea at
the same time as Christianity first came to Rome. Even a century
later, in 1698, Peter the Great created a Russian Order of knighthood,
the Knights of the Blue Ribbon whose emblem was the St Andrew's
Cross.

The Saltire Flag

The Saltire (Cross of St Andrew) is essentially a dynamic community icon, its diagonals expressing radical and restless movement to all four points of the compass – in contrast to the more static finality of the so-called 'Latin' cross with its 90 degree quarterings.

The word 'Saltire' comes from the Old French *saultoir*, itself derived from the Low Latin *saltatorium* – a stirrup, from the Latin *saltare*, to leap, presumably into the saddle. Like many English words, it has a long family tree, denoting much movement geographically, motivated by commerce, culture and war. It is a word which above all denotes action.

The saltire is the Scottish National Flag and Arms, defined by Act of Parliament as Azure (sky blue), a Saltire Argent (silver). This is recorded in the Lyon Register (1672) as the 'Armes or Badge' proper and peculiar to the Kingdom of Scotland.

Although the flag and colours of Scotland are habitually rendered as white, the correct heraldic colour of the saltire is silver (argent). As silver paint tarnishes easily and silver thread is expensive, white is substituted. But it should be noted that the colour white does not exist in heraldry – it is merely the representation of silver metal. As for the background of the saltire – the Royal Navy uses dark blue (Pantone 549C8771B) rather than Azure or sky blue (Pantone 300) because it weathers better. On 17 February 2003 the Scottish Parliament, responding to a petition from retired accountant George Reid, recommended that the colour of the saltire flag should be Sky Blue (Pantone 300).[33]

The Cross of St Andrew is the flag which any Scotsman is entitled to fly, or wear as a badge, the emblem of his national identity and the focus of his patriotism. It is also the proper flag to fly in Scottish churches.

One major problem in examining the use of the saltire is the scarcity of Scottish heraldic records, many of which have not survived. Some were burnt at a fire in Perth in 1650 when the Lyon King, Sir James Balfour, was removing them for safety before the arrival of Oliver Cromwell. A second fire about 20 years later is believed to have destroyed the register at the Lyon Office. In addition, some 85 hogsheads of Scottish historical papers were lost at sea in 1661 while they were on their way back to Scotland from London where they had been taken by General George Monck.

The burgh crosses of Scotland, which date back to the time of

William the Lion, were often decorated with the saltire – this was the case in Inverness, Burntisland and Dunfermline, for example. In many cases the saltire would be displayed on a shield held by a unicorn.

One of the clearest statements of the importance of the saltire to the Scots is found in the Acts of Parliament of Robert II (1 July 1385). A treaty between the kings of Scotland and France agreed that every Frenchman or Scot should wear a white St Andrew's Cross on his chest and on his back. If his jacket or his coat was white, he was required to wear the white cross on a piece of black cloth which could either be round or square. Black was specified rather than blue, presumably to give the maximum contrast with the white jackets of the French. A similar order was issued in 1523. Hence, the saltire was also a very functional symbol.

The St Andrew's Cross was also used in naval warfare. Some of the naval commanders proudly bore the name of 'Andrew' and feature prominently in the history of Scotland's navy. The Great Michael, a ship built for of James IV in 1511, was said to have been 73 metres in length, with 35 big guns and 300 small artillery. It was capable of carrying 300 sailors, 120 gunners and 1,000 soldiers. This giant man-of-war, said at the time to be the largest warship in the world, was commanded by Sir Andrew Wood of Largo (1460-1540). For its construction, most of the trees of Fife were reported to have been cut down. The main standard of the vessel was the St Andrew's Cross on a blue background.

In hard-fought sea battles, Sir Andrew Barton, commander of the Lion and a former pirate, destroyed many English ships. Finally, he lost both his ships in an engagement with Sir Edward Howard whom Henry VIII had sent against him. As he lay dying in 1511, Barton encouraged his men with the words:

> 'Fight on, my men' Sir Andrew says,
> 'And never flinch before the foe,
> And stand fast by St Andrew's Cross,
> Until you hear my whistle blow'.

Although the cross of St Andrew was silver on a blue background, it might be displayed over any colour or mixture of colours – in the 1540s ships' ensigns were flown with white crosses over the royal colours of red and yellow. It is worth noting that, in England, the white saltire on a red background is also the Neville family arms.

But, later, James VI (King James I of England 1603-25) issued a proclamation to his naval forces that 'our subjects of North Britain shall wear in their foretops the white cross only as they were accustomed'. The *Accounts of the Lord High Treasurer* for August 1513 record the fever of activity with which the Scots prepared for the Battle of Flodden. Not only were cloth and fringes ordered but extra payments were made to expedite the contract ('Item for making of them in haste 4/-').

Several Scottish battle standards survive. The Douglas Standard was said to have been carried at the Battle of Otterburn (1388) by Archibald Douglas, second Earl of Douglas. It is of green silk with a number of devices painted onto the cloth, one being a white St Andrew's Cross, now oxidised to black. The Marchmont Standard seems to have been the flag of the Warden of the Marches in the 16th century. It bears a St Andrew's Cross, as does the 'Blue Blanket' of Edinburgh, said to have been given to the Incorporated Trades of the city by James III and his queen, Margaret. The flag of the Incorporated Trades of Stirling is light blue and displays a white saltire.

The saltire flag appears at many key moments in Scottish history: during the Battle of Carberry Hill (1567) the forces of Mary Queen of Scots displayed the saltire; at the siege of Edinburgh Castle in 1572-73, both the defender, Kirkaldy of Grange and the Regent Morton flew the saltire!

After the Reformation, there was an understandable decline in interest in saints and their feast days. However, even John Knox's Liturgy – the Book of Common Order, still lists the names of many saints.

The saltire also featured in political events where the stamp of tradition was required. In 1621, a charter granted under the Great Seal of Scotland, was given to Sir William Alexander to begin the colonisation of Nova Scotia. The ensigns armorial of this colony consisted of a silver shield with a blue St Andrew's Cross. Eight years later, the king authorised the Scottish Baronets of Nova Scotia to wear a personal decoration with the same blue saltire.

Whether they were Roman Catholics serving the King of France or Protestants fighting for Gustavus Adolphus (with his four Scottish generals and 22 Scottish colonels), Scots always carried the saltire. The Douglas regiment which entered the service of Louis XIII of France in 1634 (later the 1st Royal Scots), also bore the Scottish national flag.

So even after the Reformation, the religious significance of the saltire was not forgotten and the flag of the Apostle came to symbolise the distinct Scottish identity common to all Scots. When in 1639, the Scots (incensed by King Charles I's attempts to introduce an alien English style of worship into Scotland) prepared to fight against the king, it is recorded that every captain in the Scottish army had 'a colour with the Scottish arms and an inscription in golden letters: FOR CHRIST'S CROWN AND COVENANT.' After the Scots were defeated at Preston (1648) and Dunbar (1650), many of their flags were captured by the English. Of the 223 flags which fell into the hands of the English and were recorded in drawings now in the British Museum, no less than 150 featured the saltire.

At state funerals the saltire was given a place of honour. At the funeral of Mary Queen of Scots, of James VI and of Oliver Cromwell, the saltire was prominently displayed. In Cromwell's case, it is described as 'Azure, a Saltire Argent'.

At sea the saltire continued to be a provocation to the English. In 1639, for example, a Scottish ship was arrested in the Thames for hanging out the 'Scotch flag of St Andrew'.

The Order of the Thistle, revived during the reign of James VII, had been previously known as the Order of St Andrew. On the badge of the Order there appears the figure of the saint in a green gown and purple surcoat, carrying a white enamelled cross. The Star of the Order is a silver saltire with rays radiating from the arms, echoing the blinding vision of the morning sun seen by King Angus and his army at Athelstaneford many years before.

Today, the ribbon of the Order is green, from the colour of the Thistle. The original colours were those of the national flag – blue and white. The Jewel, worn by the Dean of the Order is oval in shape and carries a plain saltire. It belonged to James VII (1633-1701). In the centre of the Jewel is an oval of chalcedony cut with a cameo of St Andrew and his cross. The figure of the saint is white, while the background is a bluish grey.

However, the revival of the Order in 1688 did not meet with universal approval. Describing the events, Gilbert Burnett, (1643-1715), Bishop of Salisbury, wrote: 'They broke into all popish chapels, and into the church of Holy Rood House, which had been adorned at a great charge to be a royal chapel, particularly for the Order of St Andrew and the Thistle'.

In the field of commerce, Scots also used the image of St Andrew. In one of the most ill-fated of their ventures five ships of the

Company of Scotland trading to Africa and the Indies (The Darien Scheme) sailed from Leith on 17 July 1698. One of the armed ships was the St Andrew. At their arrival on the Isthmus of Panama, the Scots constructed Fort St Andrew for their colony of New Caledonia. More successful were the Scottish financial institutions at home. The saltire was traditionally prominent in the arms of the Edinburgh Merchant Company (founded 1693), the Company of Linen Manufacturers of Scotland (1694), the Bank of Scotland (1695) and the Royal Bank of Scotland (1727). It is also prominent in the crest of the Royal College of Surgeons of Edinburgh (1505), the Writers to Her Majesty's Signet (1532) and the Society of Antiquaries of Scotland (1780). Many historic regiments proudly displayed the saltire – the Royal Scots, the King's Own Scottish Borderers, the Black Watch, the Highland Light Infantry, the Gordon Highlanders and the Cameron Highlanders. The Queen's Bodyguard for Scotland, the Royal Company of Archers also carry the figure of St Andrew on his cross.

After the Union of the Parliaments in 1707, the St Andrew's Cross was to some degree supplanted by the Union Flag. However, during the 1715 Jacobite Uprising, the saltire came back into prominence. Lady Kenmure had embroidered her husband's blue flag with a golden saltire when he led his men from Galloway to fight for the Old Pretender. The saltire was also flown by an Edinburgh volunteer unit on the government side, using a flag said to have been carried at the Battle of Bothwell Brig (1679).

It is interesting to note that even for Jacobites politically exiled abroad, St Andrew maintained his position as spiritual lynchpin of the Scottish nation. On 30 November 1717, for example, although exiled in Italy, the Old Pretender, Prince James Francis Edward Stewart – 'James III' – made a conscious effort to go to the evening service of Benediction at the church of St Andrew the Apostle in Urbino in Italy to fulfil the obligations of the holy-day:

> As the morning of that day was the Festival of the Apostle and His Majesty had made his devotions, because the said Saint is the Protector of Scotland, that evening he did not hold a reception.

At the Battle of Culloden, the final act of the 1745 Rising, the Appin Clan regiment's colours escaped the conflict. It was made from light blue silk with a *yellow* saltire. In Edinburgh, the flag used from 1676-

1789 by the first company of the City Trained Bands was a white saltire on a blue background.

Over in the United States, the flag of the American Colonies, with its 13 stripes and the old Union Flag in the corner, had the English part of the Union Flag removed in 1777, leaving the Scottish colours. One of the flags used by the Confederate side in the American Civil War had its stars arranged in the form of the St Andrew Cross (the Southern Cross – Gules, on a saltire azure).

Seals

The wax seals used to authenticate official documents on the Scottish heraldic records that have survived, reveal a considerable amount about the symbolism and self-image of Scotland.

Since it is a general principle of heraldry that a simpler form precedes a more complex one, it is perhaps safe to assume that the stylised and non-representational saltire was used as a symbol before the crucified figure of St Andrew was adopted.

The saltire or the symbol from which it was derived (Constantine's *Chi Rho*) would probably have been in use in north of the Border before the first known representation in Scotland of Saint Andrew crucified. This can be seen on the Seal of the Guardians of Scotland (1286-92), where it is accompanied by the motto: 'Andrew, be the leader of your compatriots, the Scots', probably suggesting that the saltire or a painted version of it was often carried by the Scots into battle.

In due course, however, the human figure of the crucified saint replaced the simple X of the Chi Rho. In the 13th century, the seal of Bishop Gamelin, chaplain to Alexander III and Chancellor of Scotland (1254), shows St Andrew being tied to his cross. Bishop William Fraser's seal, (Chancellor 1274-80), has the Apostle tied by his arms to a saltire cross. That of James Bane (Bishop of St Andrews 1328-32), elaborates the image by having St Andrew lashed to his cross by four men, two of them climbing up on ladders to tie his arms to the wood.

Although the Thistle as a badge for Scotland dates from the reign of James III (1488-1513), the saltire is the authentic badge for the Scottish nation. It appears on the seals of James I and James II and on that of Queen Mary of Gueldres, founder of Trinity College, Edinburgh. In the 15th century also, a saltire features on the seal of the vicar-general of St Andrews.

Post-Reformation seals of the dioceses of St Andrews, Dunblane,

Caithness and Edinburgh, all carry the saltire. It is worth noting that two English cathedral sees, dedicated to St Andrew, display the saltire as part of their arms – Rochester and Wells. The badge of the Conservator of Scottish Privileges in the Netherlands (an office dating from before 1444) contains a small shield with the figure of St Andrew. From the middle of the 14th century, the same figure of Saint Andrew was being used by the Scottish students' union at the University of Orleans.

Even at a later period, when Oliver Cromwell set aside the rule of the king, St Andrew is officially recognised as the symbol of Scotland: an order was made on 22 April 1654 that 'the Arms of Scotland, viz, a cross commonly called St Andrew's Cross' should be carried by all public seals, seals of office and seals of bodies civil or corporate in Scotland.

Coins

Early Scottish coins usually have the head of the sovereign on one side and a cross (sometimes a saltire), on the other. David II (1329-71) issued the first Scottish gold coin – the *noble* – with a St Andrew's Cross on the reverse. The Scottish *noble* is a direct copy of a similar English coin which bears the Cross of St George. This is also evidence that at this period the saltire was used as a national emblem to differentiate Scotland from England.

A series of coins issued by succeeding Scottish kings were known as 'St Andrews' from the saltire and the saint on the reverse. Gold crowns of James V (1513-42) carry on the obverse a royal shield with a saltire on each side, perhaps symbolising the support of the king by the people; while the bawbee of this period displays a saltire with a royal crown at the junction of the arms.

Gold crowns of Mary Queen of Scots (1542-67) are closely modelled on those of her father, James V. The £6 piece of James VI (1567-1625), however, carries a sword and sceptre in the form of a St Andrew's Cross. The saltire *plack* (coin) also has two crossed sceptres. In the British Army the Grenadier Guards still carry the sword and sceptre crossed in this way as a regimental badge. It is described as a device used by the House of Stuart.

It is interesting to note the papal arms on the scabbard of the Scottish Sword of State. A gift from Pope Julius II to King James IV, it was presented to the king at Holyrood on Easter Sunday 1507. Between the three-tiered crown and the papal shield are the symbolic keys of papal authority, crossed saltire-fashion and wrapped with crisscross bindings, recalling the Roman imperial fasces, symbolic of authority and retribution.[34]

From the Union of the Crowns (1603), coins issued by the Scottish Mint rarely carried any national emblems, perhaps out of sensitivity to the unifying aspirations of the monarch now based in London. In 1626, the Scottish Privy Council noted that the seals for use in Scotland carried the Royal Arms quartered in the English manner and ordered them to be broken and new ones made. Two centuries later, the Royal Arms (which carried the English three leopards in the place of honour), displayed on Edinburgh's General Post Office were removed at the instigation of the Lyon Depute and the Usher of the White Rod as 'derogatory to the independence of Scotland'.

Some of the copper coins of Charles I and Charles II had the four national shields diplomatically arranged to form a saltire. Among the coins issued by James VII was a ten-shilling piece with a St Andrew's Cross on the reverse. Broadly speaking, the Royal Arms of Scotland have continued to be used in the coinage of the realm by the Houses of Stewart, of Hanover and of Windsor.

Sculpture, Architecture and Painting

In painting, sculpture and stained glass St Andrew was often seen as an old bald man with one or two books in his hand – perhaps recalling the *Acts of Andrew*. Traditionally he is presented as a fisherman with fish, a fishing-net or a rope, or sometimes with a boat. In Greece St Andrew was seen as the founder of the Byzantine patriarchate as distinct from the Roman papacy founded by Peter – but only the Greek and Syriac churches recognised this claim. The apocryphal *Acts of Andrew* were used by the heretical Gnostics and Manicheans to oppose the mainstream canonical teaching of the New Testament and it was from the elaborate adventures in the *Acts of Andrew* that the image of St Andrew's crucifixion was taken, not from the *Acts of the Apostles* or other parts of the New Testament.

St Andrew makes a relatively late appearance in Christian art. In the Greek East only his crucifixion is shown; in the Latin West, an edited, less exaggerated version of the *Acts of Andrew* was used as source-material. In the Afro-Asian churches, however, a wealth of miracle stories surround the life of the saint. There, from earliest times, the Apostle was unashamedly used as a vehicle for moral teaching.

The earliest series of crucifixions show not the X-shaped cross, but the familiar Latin cross as used in the crucifixion of Jesus. A fifth-century Egyptian catacomb also preserves the image of St Andrew and St

Philip feeding the 5,000. From the sixth century onward, St Andrew's dishevelled white hair and beard are instantly recognisable. He is often shown directing the feeding of the multitude and – as in the mosaics from the church of San Apollinare Nuovo in Ravenna – with Peter at the moment of their calling.

A head of St Andrew dating from the eighth century can be found in the ruined church of Santa Maria Antiqua in the Forum in Rome. By the ninth century, St Andrew appears in a number of Byzantine painted miniatures in manuscripts – such as the *Codex of Homilies* of Gregory of Nazianus or a Greek calendar of saints (*menologion*) now in the Vatican Library. On both these miniatures, St Andrew is shown nailed to his cross. It is in ninth century Byzantine manuscripts that the first series of crucifixions of St Andrew show him on the Latin cross, nailed but not tied (contrary to the description in the *Acts of Andrew*), with others present to witness his final agony.

St Andrew on a Latin cross appears on a hymn book (a *troparium*) from Autun in Burgundy in central France, probably made in the tenth century. During that and the succeeding century, in the margins of prayer books of the psalms (*psalters*) St Andrew is depicted preaching and baptising. He also appears among other saints on carved ivories of this period. In a service book (*sacramentary*) at Ivrea in northern Italy made about the year 1,000, St Andrew is shown in the centre of the picture, on a Latin cross, while to his left stands a military executioner tying him to it.

On the 11th-century bronze doors of the basilica of St Paul outside the Walls (San Paolo fuori le Mure) in Rome, St Andrew is depicted nailed to Y-shaped cross. From the 12th century dates a statue of St Andrew at Amalfi, Italy while in 13th-century glass paintings at Troyes and Auxerre in France, St Andrew is shown chasing away demons in the shape of dogs.

Images of St Andrew in the 15th century include those painted by Hugo van der Goes (died 1482) who painted the magnificent 'Trinity Altarpiece' showing King James III of Scotland being presented by St Andrew, a work at present on loan from Her Majesty the Queen and exhibited in the National Gallery of Scotland at the Mound in Edinburgh. Papal recognition of the importance of St Andrew to the Scots can still be seen today in the sceptre which forms part of the Honours of Scotland. Presented to James IV by Pope Alexander in 1494, its complex design includes a statuette of St Andrew with his cross.

Many of the greatest Renaissance painters chose to include St

Andrew in their work – Fra Angelico (1387-1455), Andrea Mantegna (1431-1506), Tintoretto (1518-94), El Greco (1541-1614) all used St Andrew in their compositions. The best-known image of St Andrew is perhaps that in Leonardo da Vinci's (1452-1519) 'Last Supper' (1497), painted on the wall of Santa Maria delle Grazie, Milan, where St Andrew can be seen sitting third from the left end of the table.

One of Leonardo's best-known anatomical studies is the pen and ink drawing of the 'Vitruvian Man', a drawing from around 1485-90 of a nude male figure standing and stretching out his arms in a T-formation inside an inscribed square and then repeating the movement with his arms raised and his legs spread out inside a circle in what is virtually the familiar X-cross of St Andrew. The drawing was made to illustrate a passage in *De Architectura*, the only surviving Roman treatise on architecture, written by Marcus Vitruvius Pollio, an architect and military engineer in the service of the Emperor Augustus. By Leonardo's time, the 'Cosmological Man' was a traditional figure of astrological importance. For Leonardo, man was a microcosm of the universe, the human body being constructed on a framework of a square and a circle. All architecture was, for Leonardo as for the architects of Classical Greece, based on the harmonious proportions of the human body, the Golden Section upon which the designs of their finest temples were based.

Germany in the 16th century also found St Andrew a significant figure, as can be seen in the anonymous painting (now in the National Galleries of Scotland) of the saint with the donor's wife and children. In the USA a fine wood carving of St Andrew by Tilman Riemenschneider (c1460-1531) is on display in the Samuel H Kress Collection at the Atlanta Art Association Galleries, Atlanta, Georgia. One of the best-known 17th-century paintings of the Apostle is 'The Martyrdom of St Andrew' by Bartholomé Murillo (1617-82), now in Madrid.

Paradoxically, considering that St Andrew was once used by the Patriarchs of Constantinople as a means of rivalling the status of Rome, it is in Rome that many of the major monuments associated with the Apostle are to be found. For sheer size, it is the colossal statue of St Andrew in St Peter's, Rome that catches the eye. It was carved around 1629 by the Flemish sculptor François Duquesnoy after he and Gian Bernini had completed the canopy (*baldachino*) which stands in front of one of the four great piers supporting the dome of St Peter's.

Lovers of music will recall that it was in 1678 at Sant' Andrea delle

Fratte on the Via Capo le Case, that the composer Alessandro Scarlatti (1659-1725) was married. In medieval times, Sant' Andrea delle Fratte had been a resting-place for Scottish pilgrims. The staff wore purple, hence the purple soutanes of Scots students at the Pontifical Scots College today. Sant' Andrea delle Fratte has a long association with pilgrims from Scotland and was in more recent times the Roman church of the late Cardinal Thomas Winning, Archbishop of Glasgow. In the church are large and dramatic mural paintings of the death of St Andrew (Lazzaro Baldi) and the Crucifixion of St Andrew (GB Leonardi). In similar vein at Sant' Andrea al Quirinale (built by Gian Bernini in 1678) can be seen a high altarpiece of the Crucifixion of St Andrew by Guillaume Courtois (1628-79).

In 1461 the head of St Andrew, preserved inside a silver-gilt reliquary was brought to Italy. It had been removed from the Church of St Andrew in Patras the previous year. It was conveyed by the brother of the Despot of Morea, Thomas Palaeologus, and then brought to Rome in 1462. The Byzantine reliquary was a primitive, elongated egg-shaped head with bearded features in very low relief, surmounted by a gem-studded metal garland. The reliquary was in two halves, hinged at the back of the skull. After it was returned to the Orthodox Church by Pope Pius VI in 1962, it was replaced by a less representational reliquary, shaped like a church and more in keeping with current Orthodox belief and practice.

A pen and ink drawing attributed to Ventura Salimbeni depicts the scene when Pius II received St Andrew's head at the Milvian Bridge. Today the drawing is preserved in Florence at the Museo Horne. In addition, three marble reliefs by Paolo Romano showing two angels supporting St Andrew's head are in the Grotte Vaticane, Rome. From Paolo Romano's sculptures and his statue of St Andrew standing outside Sant'Andrea al Ponte Milvio, it is clear that the head was transferred from the original Greek silver gilt reliquary to Simone da Firenze's silver gilt reliquary for the public reception of the head by Pius II. Da Firenze's reliquary is highly realistic but also heavily ornamented. It stands on substantial shoulders set above a broad decorated base. Behind the head is fixed a sunburst set inside a halo. There is a carrying-handle shaped like a sword-fish on each shoulder. Today, the reliquary can be seen in Pienza, at the Museo del Duomo. The church of Sant' Andrea al Ponte Milvio was erected by Pius II in 1462 on the spot where he met Cardinal Bessarion who handed over the head of St Andrew brought by Thomas Palaeologus from

Constantinople. The church was remodelled in the 15th century by Pope Nicholas V (who added the watchtowers) and was restored in 1805 by Pius VII, who commissioned Valdier to erect the triumphal arch at the entrance. Blown up by Garibaldi to prevent the advance of the French, it was again restored in 1850 by Pius IX.

Sant' Andrea della Valle, built in 1591 from a design by Francisco Grimaldi and Giacomo della Porta, is especially associated with the Piccolomini family. At the end of its nave are the monumental tombs to two popes of the Piccolomini family, including Pius II and Pius III. The Theatine Order's church and convent of Sant' Andrea della Valle had been founded 20 years earlier on the site of the Piccolomini palace. The Palazzo di Siena, as it was popularly called, had been built by Cardinal Piccolomini between 1460 and 1472. It had since been the headquarters of the Piccolomini family in Rome.

In 1582 it passed into the hands of Costanza, the widowed Duchess of Amalfi, descended through her father from Pius II's nephew Andrea. Costanza was the last of her line. The Duchy of Amalfi had already passed into other hands and in 1610 she herself died at a convent in Naples.

The painter Domenichino (1581-1641) filled the apse of Sant' Andrea delle Valle with key scenes from the life of St Andrew – John the Baptist pointing out Jesus to Andrew; Jesus calling Andrew; the executioners torturing Andrew; Andrew worshipping the Cross; Andrew being carried to Heaven by the angels.

In 1610 the Chapel of St Andrew in St Peter's Basilica was demolished by Pope Paul V to make room for his new construction at St Peter's. However, the actual bodies of the two Piccolomini popes were not transferred to Sant' Andrea della Valle until 1623. The marble reliefs from the tomb of Aeneas Sylvius Piccolomini, later Pius II (1405-64) are attributed to Paolo Romano.

Sant' Andrea della Via Flaminia, a small round church constructed by Jacopo Vignola (1550-55), was erected by Pope Julius III to commemorate his deliverance from Charles V's soldiers at the Sack of Rome in 1527.

San Spirito in Sassia was founded in AD 726 for the comfort of Saxon pilgrims by Ine, King of Wessex, who himself died in Rome the same year. Part of the arm of St Andrew was given by Pius II to San Spirito in Sassia. In 1540 the church was rebuilt by Sangallo the Younger.

San Gregorio Magno on the Coelian Hill was originally built by Gregory the Great on the site of his father's house and dedicated to

St Andrew. It was in the church in AD 596 that St Augustine bade farewell to St Gregory before setting out to convert England. A new church dedicated to St Gregory was rebuilt in the 17th and 18th centuries. In the centre of the church is the Chapel of Sant' Andrea with paintings of the Flagellation of St Andrew by Domenichino and St Andrew on the road to his Cross by Guido Reni. There also, in the chapel of Santa Barbara, is a fresco by Antonio Viviani (1602) depicting the famous 'Non angli sed angeli' incident which led to the Augustinian mission to England.

St Andrew's Church of Scotland, Rome, on the Via XX Settembre, one of ten charges within the Presbytery of Europe, was founded in 1862 by Scots and Americans. The Revd David Huie, at that time Minister of St Andrew's, explained that:

> There is no St Andrew's Society or Caledonian Society in Rome. We have a St Andrew's service on the Sunday nearest to St Andrew's Day to which the British ambassador and representatives of the Scots College are invited. We usually follow this with a congregational lunch. On one occasion a couple of years ago our efforts to advertise this service with a notice: 'Are there any Scots out there in Rome?' appeared as 'Are there any Scouts out there in Rome?' The original question remained unanswered.
>
> The Pontifical Scots College, Rome (founded by Pope Clement VIII in 1600) normally marks St Andrew's Day with a Mass in the present College chapel, followed by a lunch. In 1995, the Mass was held in Sant' Andrea delle Fratte. The congregation was addressed by the Very Revd Professor Bob Davidson and the then new Cardinal Thomas Winning was guest of honour at the Scots College lunch which followed.

Today, Scotland's capital city also has its national shrine of St Andrew, a side chapel with a life-size wooden statue of the saint and a newly commissioned golden icon hanging over the altar, with the saltire woven into the decorated carpet below. In brightly lit enclosures within the altar-stone are two relics of St Andrew, mounted in gold.

The first was brought from Italy by John Patrick, 3rd Marquess of Bute, a gift of the Archbishop of Amalfi in 1879 to Archbishop John

The head of St Andrew carried in procession through Patras, Greece. (Courtesy of Panteleimon Hadjiioannu)

Strain, metropolitan of the recently restored Roman Catholic Scottish hierarchy. The marquess also presented a small relic of St Andrew to the church of St James in St Andrews, Fife. Another relic was presented by Pope Paul VI to Cardinal Gordon Joseph Gray to celebrate his elevation to the College of Cardinals (1969). Pope Paul VI, in an ecumenical gesture had earlier (1964) returned relics of St Andrew to Patras in Greece where, in a special reliquary at St Andrew's Church, they hold a special place of honour and devotion.

Contemporary Art

It is possible to identify some innovative examples of the saltire, even in 20th-century art such as Josef Hartwig's Bauhaus chess set. Made from lacquered wood, it was mass-produced from 1923. The shape of each piece was determined by its move. The bishop is represented by a deep saltire cut out of the square black chess piece. The saltire indicates the way in which the bishop moves – diagonally with reference to the edge of the board. The chess set was very popular and every set, made from pear wood in natural and black finishes, was carved by hand.

In *The Radiant City* (1933) the revolutionary French architect Le Corbusier observes:

> Human creation is a work of art. On the one hand, nature: a cone opening away from us towards infinity. Its point transfixes us; its contents are always flowing into us ... On the other hand, another cone, also opening away towards infinity: human creation. Between the two cones, where their points meet, stands man. Man the perceiver and man the revealer: the focal point.

This is the significance also of the saltire.

11
Saints Abroad

Saint David

The time has come to compare and contrast the national patron saints of the British Isles. They are St David (Wales), St George (England), St Patrick (Ireland) and St Andrew (Scotland). St David was born around AD 542 at Menevia (now St Davids) to parents of royal stock. David was educated by the finest local teachers and grew in learning and authority until the time came when he was ordained a priest.

In a valley near Whitesands Bay, David was able to set up his first monastic community and build his first church. Living in beehive-shaped stone cells, David and his fellow monks worked in the fields, prayed and studied from morning until sunset, also caring for the sick and for pilgrims.[35] He was consecrated archbishop, being chosen as primate of the Cambrian Church after the Synod of Brefi (c.AD 545) where he had denounced the then-fashionable Pelagian heresy (which claimed that man was responsible for his own sins and for his own salvation, and so did not need the help of God).

St David, around whom many legends were woven, died around AD 589, on the first day in March – on which his memory is now annually celebrated in Wales and throughout the world where Welsh people gather.

St David's body is thought to have been buried at the cathedral in St Davids. He was canonised in 1120 by Pope Callixtus II – who dedicated the cathedral to St David and St Andrew. The cathedral and its relics of St David became an important focus of pilgrimage. However, it was not until the 16th century that St David was widely recognised as the patron saint of Wales.

Saint George

St George (from the Greek for 'land-worker') is thought to have been an officer in the Roman army who converted to Christianity and was tortured and beheaded in Palestine around AD 304. He was widely regarded as a model of chivalry and his gruesome torture, enthusiastically and vividly elaborated by medieval artists, highlights the conflict between the religions of the Classical world and Christianity.[36] St George defeats the dragon and saves the maiden: he is sometimes taken to be a symbol of rebirth – the conquest of winter by spring. The first reference to St George as patron saint of England is in 1351. Although in 1969 St George's Day was downgraded in status by the Roman Catholic Church to an optional local feast, the recent reclamation of St George as patron saint of England reflects to some extent the arrival of devolution for Wales and Scotland and also a growing awareness that 'Britain' and 'England' are two distinct (but overlapping) entities. St George's Day (also known as 'Shakespeare's Birthday') is celebrated annually on 23 April.

Saint Patrick

Patrick was born, probably in what is today Strathclyde in Scotland (or perhaps in Wales) sometime between AD 387-90. When he was about 16 years old Patrick is thought to have been captured on mainland Britain and taken to Ireland where he was soon sold as a slave. He spent six years working as a shepherd, an occupation which gave him plenty of time to meditate and pray until the time came when he was ordered in a dream to return to mainland Britain. Patrick duly escaped and began a series of visits to monasteries in Europe to educate himself in Theology and Scripture.[37] He was later sent by Pope Celestine to convert England to Christianity, and then to repeat the process in Ireland, being conveyed by his assistants in a horse-driven chariot. St Patrick is said to have completed the conversion of Ireland in 33 years, leaving monasteries which preserved and developed culture and learning. St Patrick died around AD 462 at Saul in County Down. Following St Patrick's long ministry, Ireland became known as the 'Land of Saints'.

Patron Saints and National Identity

Today there are strong but differing views on national patron saints. Gwenllian Lansdown, in 2006 the Information Officer for Plaid Cymru described the national and international fervour which grips the Welsh psyche every March: 'This year on March 1st, the seat of democracy in Wales – the *Senedd* (Assembly) – was officially opened, heralding a new beginning in Welsh politics. On St David's Day, across Wales, children in schools will compete in Eisteddfodau and concerts. They usually wear traditional dress or Wales rugby or football shirts. There may be dinners, concerts or gigs held in celebration of St David and this year, the second annual St David's Day Parade was held in Cardiff.'

Leek soup and Welsh cakes are traditional culinary favourites. Plaid Cymru believes that St David's Day should be a national bank holiday and has been campaigned as such. In 2006, in a poll for St David's Day, more than 80% of Welsh people said it should to be a bank holiday. However, the following year, a petition for this was rejected by the office of the Prime Minister. New York, Moscow and other cities across the globe have had St David's Day celebrations.

But there were also some firmly opposite views: Euro-MP Eluned Morgan (Labour) warned that if St David's Day became a national holiday its meaning would be lost. She feared that if 1 March was a bank holiday, children would not attend school and there would accordingly be little incentive to arrange appropriate community celebrations such as schools put on now.

Writing on 'Religion and National Identity' historian Robert Hope points out that Welsh life and culture is 'diverse and pluralistic' and draws the parallel in the almost identical timing of votes in Wales and Scotland in favour (respectively) of an assembly and a parliament.[38] He also underlines the importance of a collective memory of a common past, noting that 'The past is always important, even when it is re-appropriated through myth. In the same volume, Dr E Wyn James also points to the 'continued interweaving' of Christianity in Welsh culture and identity.[39]

In England, St George's Day and Shakespeare's Birthday in 2005 saw more than 9,000 people thronging the Globe Theatre in London for a free family event where activities included the opportunity to declaim some of the bard's finest lines from the world-famous Elizabethan stage. Covent Garden's free family day (organised by the Royal Society of St George in collaboration with St George's Day Events) offered displays of Morris Dancing, English folk dance and song and a Punch and Judy show. There was also a short service, wreath-laying and a march-past at the Cenotaph as well as a gathering of sporting heroes and fans in Trafalgar Square to make a clear statement that England was a nation opposed to racism and London was an ideal location for the 2012 Olympic Games – an astute mixture of culture and politics.

The reluctance of the English authorities to make 23 April a public holiday, however, infuriated some, such as 47-year-old Tony Bennett, licensee of The Otter in Thorpe Marriott, Norfolk. Magistrates had refused to grant him an hour's extension the previous April, arguing that 23 April was not a 'special occasion,' so Mr Bennett took his complaint to the High Court of Justice. However, in spite of Mr Bennett's legal representative quoting the memorable lines 'Cry God for Harry, England and Saint George', from Shakespeare's Henry V, the High Court judge remained unmoved.[40]

However, St George's Day has been widely celebrated since at least the 18th century by Englishmen abroad. The St George's Society of New York was founded by Englishmen living in New York in 1770 to celebrate St George's Day and to assist fellow countrymen in distress. It is one of the rare American institutions predating the Revolutionary War still functioning today.

St George's Society of New York, Annual Dinner, 23 April 1857. Founded in 1770 to assist those born under the British flag who fell into desperate straits in New York.

Despite the American Revolution and the War of 1812, the society quietly carried out its charitable mission, ranging from the protection of poor British immigrants in the 1830s, 40s and 50s to aiding English war brides in the two World Wars. Along the way, it advocated the establishment of an Anglo-American church, a hospital, and a cemetery in New York City for needy British subjects; and acted as an employment agency during depressions and times of hardship.

In the early days of the society membership was limited exclusively to natives of England but it soon grew to include anyone from the United Kingdom, the British Commonwealth, and now even the United States. In recent years the membership has become predominantly American, but it also includes people who merely have some affinity with the United Kingdom.

In recognition of its English origins the society was honoured in

1999 to receive full armorial bearings from the College of Arms in London. It is one of relatively few American entities to have been granted arms. In 2000 HRH The Duke of Gloucester, consented to become the society's first royal patron, thus further linking the society with the British crown and the royal family. In 2003 he visited the society's office, met with some of its beneficiaries, and took tea with the members at a reception held in his honour on 15 October.

In past decades the society has taken a lead role in creating greater awareness of Britain's presence and contribution to New York City. In 2001 The British in New York since 1770 exhibit at the New York Historical Society drew attention to the many cultural, artistic and commercial links between New York and Great Britain.

In 2003 the society, in partnership with the British Consulate-General in New York and with the full support of the City of New York's Parks & Recreation Department, embarked upon its biggest project in years: the creation of the British Memorial Garden at Hanover Square in Lower Manhattan. The garden, conceived as a gift from the British community to New York, was designed by a well-known British landscape architect, and would make Hanover Square a destination for all. It would also serve as a public space for Remembrance Day observations and commemorate the British and Commonwealth subjects who died on 9/11.

In Canada, the origins of the St George's Society of Toronto go back to 1834 when local newspapers reported that a group of loyal and enthusiastic citizens celebrated St George's Day with an elegant dinner at the British Coffee House, at King and York Streets, and decided to form the St George's Society of Toronto. It was founded as an immigrant aid organisation and became famous in the city's early years, particularly in the 1800s and early part of the 1900s, for providing food, money and medical services for the city's poor and unfortunate.

Although it was started as a benevolent organization to help people of English origin it never limited itself to providing help to the needy. The society offered help to anyone who qualified for assistance. Over the years, some of the city's most influential and important leaders in politics, business, education, the arts and philanthropy have been members.

Today, membership is open to men and women of all cultures who have an interest in getting together to further the English traditions that have helped Toronto become the enviable place it is in which to live.

In general, however, annual celebrations in memory of national patron saints may sometimes create tensions between the demands of national identity and those of commercial exploitation. This and many other issues surrounding St Patrick's Day are teased out in Mike Cronin and Daryl Adair's *The Wearing of the Green* (London: Routledge, 2002).

Ironically, as in the case of Scotland, the Irish national saint's day hardly rates a mention in the work of the country's greatest literary figures – Jonathan Swift, Oscar Wilde, James Joyce or WB Yeats, but it may well be that the celebration was so taken for granted that it was passed over without mention: among great Scottish writers St Andrew is also largely absent from the works of Robert Louis Stevenson and Robert Burns and from the diaries of Sir Walter Scott.

But, in Scott's case, at least, this is deceptive. While Sir Walter's annual journal entries for 30 November do not refer to celebrations for the national saint, Scott was clearly well aware of the traditions associated with St Andrew as he used it to great effect in his novel *Quentin Durward* (1823): 'St Andrew was the first called to Apostleship. He made many converts to Christianity and was finally crucified on a cross of peculiar form, which has since been called the St Andrew's cross. Certain of his relics were brought to Scotland in the fourth century, and he has since that time been honoured as the patron saint of that country. He is also the patron saint of the Burgundian Order, the Golden Fleece.'

Scott then goes on to make quite deliberate use of St Andrew as a powerful expression of Scottish nationhood abroad:

> But Quentin had heard words of comfort, and, exerting his strength, he suddenly shook off both the finishers of the law, and, with his arms still bound, ran to the Scottish Archer. 'Stand by me, countryman,' he said, in his own language, 'for the love of Scotland and Saint Andrew! I am innocent – I am your own native lands-man. Stand by me, as you shall answer at the last day'.

However, there are other much more debateable questions. The colour of the saltire flag of Scotland has recently been a matter of fierce dispute. In February 2003, responding to a petition submitted by retired Edinburgh accountant George Reid that the traditional heraldic azure blue of the saltire should be standardised, the Scottish Parliament's Education, Culture and Sport Committee recommended Pantone 300 as the correct colour. Nevertheless, it was also agreed by the Committee that there should not be any actual legislation on this but that it should be taken as guidance only.

Legislating for the colour of the national flag raises a number of doubts and confusions – the first historical record of the background of the Scottish colours is black. Moreover, in the earliest accounts of the Battle of Athelstaneford, the Saltire Cross is described as being seen as a bright light in the sky – there is no mention of its precise colour, of blue sky, clouds, or even jumbo-jet vapour trails![41]

Nigel Tranter

Today, the orthodox, widely-accepted popular view of what happened at the Battle of Athelstaneford goes back to the novelist Nigel Tranter who, in his novel *Kenneth* (1990), described King Angus' vision of the Cross at Athelstaneford as on an afternoon with a deep blue sky, with 'a cloud formation in the exact shape of ... a saltire cross, like the letter X, white against azure.'

Today, Tranter's commanding legacy as a novelist and knowledgeable historian has succeeded in making this graphic account the accepted version of the Vision of the Cross. But Tranter, who was married at Athelstaneford (of which he had warm and happy memories), was the first to point out that he wrote 'as a perpetrator of romantic fiction', referring to King Angus' experiences at the Battle of Athelstaneford as 'romantic stories.'[42] In essence, the heraldic saltire is a two-dimensional representation of a three-dimensional event – the battle.

However, in public life, the character of the saltire is often unknowingly misrepresented. Instead of a central light source radiating to the four corners of the flag, a 'searchlight' effect is sometimes achieved as a convenient backcloth for politicians by placing two spotlights on the ground and crossing them over a blue background. This is as misleading as the 'jumbo-jet trails' often photographed in the sky as being a true representation of the saltire, where light should radiate outwards from a central point.

Why is Tranter's 20th-century photographic realism of a pristine white cloud against a pure blue background felt to be more historically accurate than the simple and intriguing 12th-century account published by Archbishop James Ussher in 1639 – a manuscript, written by a Culdee monk at St Andrews, where the Vision of King Angus is simply a light from the sky?

The answer seems to be that Tranter had not, for reasons best known to himself, noticed the connection between the Emperor Constantine's Vision of the Cross and the Saltire.

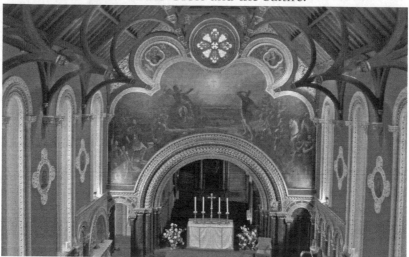

Alexander Christie's 'Vision of the Cross' (1856), a mural painting in the Chapel of St Anthony the Eremite at Murthly, Perthshire. (Courtesy of Thomas Steuart Fothringham)

The most effective image of Constantine's 'Vision of the Cross' to be found in Scotland today is the magnificent mural painted in 1856 by Alexander Christie (1807–60) in the extraordinary Chapel of St Anthony the Eremite at Murthly, on the banks of the River Tay, nine miles north of Perth. Built for Sir William George Drummond Stewart of Grandtully in 1845 and designed by James Gillespie Graham in collaboration with AWN Pugin, the chapel has as its centrepiece the mural painted across and above the arch over the altar. It shows Constantine and his army at the moment when they were dazzled by the Cross appearing high above their heads on the evening before the Battle of Milvian Bridge on AD 28 October 312.

Symbolically, behind the saltire flag is Constantine's Cross of Light and its Chi Rho of Christ Crucified that Constantine had his soldiers place on their shields and standards at the Battle of Milvian Bridge at the outskirts of Rome. The real story of the saltire is not romantic fiction.

Heraldic Confusion

For the Irish there is equally some heraldic confusion or perhaps fruitful diversity? While the colour first associated with St Patrick was blue, the cross of St Patrick in the Union flag of Great Britain is red and white. The green which today so widely symbolises Ireland and St

Patrick emerged only as late as the 17th century.

In Dublin the large number of saints' days in the Roman Catholic calendar was rationalised by the Williamite parliament of 1695 which went on to put in their place a list of only approved 29 holidays based on the Anglican traditions of the Church of Ireland.

St Patrick, however, was officially recognised, appearing on Irish coinage in the 1760s, accompanied by a shamrock. In 1783, King George III introduced an Irish honours system, the Knights of the Order of St Patrick and St Patrick's Day (17 March) continued to be celebrated, but principally by the Anglo-Irish aristocracy and wealthier classes with dinners and balls, notably at Dublin Castle. By the 1850s, however, the green of St Patrick (once shared by Protestants and Catholics alike) had developed into an almost exclusively Roman Catholic and Nationalist symbol.

Abroad, the immigrant Irish, both Protestant and Roman Catholic, had at first associated freely in the celebration of their national saint's day. This was the case in Canada during the 1830s where Irishmen of all creeds and shades of political opinion were welcomed by the local St Patrick societies. Parades in Montreal or Quebec were led by the St Patrick Society, accompanied by the St George's and St Andrew's societies, each group taking it in turn to show solidarity with the others on their respective national saint's day. Inevitably, this happy state of affairs did not last. By 1856 Montreal's Protestant Irish were forced out when the Young Men's St Patrick's Association merged with the St Patrick's Association.

It was a similar story in Melbourne, Australia. The first St Patrick's Society parades were jointly attended by Roman Catholics and Protestants who in 1843 marched and sang together but, in the very same year, two distinct and separate Irish societies emerged: the St Patrick's Society of Australia Felix and the Orange Society. The resulting sectarian tension so alarmed the authorities that it led to the Legislative Council of New South Wales passing a 'Party Processions Bill' to regulate such parades.

Scottish St Andrew's societies abroad tended to be predominantly Presbyterian or Episcopal in character, reflecting the denominational composition of the population in Scotland. This continues, broadly speaking, to be the case today with the 'Kirkin' of the Tartan'. However, the understanding of what St Andrew represents, even under a Reformed tradition (which rejects the overtly salvific function of saints in the life of the Church), still acknowledges Scotland's patron saint as having powerful apostolic authority.

The Scottish Diaspora
Societies in Scotland

Outside Scotland there are over 35 million people claiming Scottish descent. To meet the needs of Scottish ex-pats as well as Scots in the British Isles, the World Federation of Scottish Societies and individuals was formed in Edinburgh on 24 March 1959. Its aims were to maintain and preserve the rich heritage of Scotland's traditions and culture; to offer to Scots and those of Scots descent from overseas a centre of welcome and friendship from the Scots at home and to foster a closer bond of fellowship between all Scots and people of Scots descent around the world.

In Scotland itself, the St Andrew Society, a non-political body, was founded in 1907. Based in Edinburgh, it incorporated the World Federation of Scottish Societies. Its aims were to uphold the rights and privileges of the Scottish people; to secure the use of the terms and symbols (including flags) which are proper to the nation; to encourage the celebration of St Andrew's Day (30 November) as the National Day and other days of significance to Scotland; to enrich peoples' lives and strengthen the national identity by furthering the study of Scottish history and culture in all its branches; to receive into affiliation Scottish Societies at Home and Abroad in order to further the society's objects and in particular to maintain connection with people of Scottish descent.

In its ongoing campaign to encourage the celebration of St Andrew's Day its Flag Committee carried out surveys to ascertain the reaction of local councils and firms to flying the saltire on 30 November. The Scottish Flag Trust was responsible for illuminating and spotlighting the saltire and for refurbishing the memorial plaque in Athelstaneford churchyard in East Lothian as the birthplace of Scotland's flag and setting up the Flag Heritage Centre, a 4-star visitor attraction incorporating a stone dovecot built in 1583 by George Hepburn and restored in 1996. Inside, a short audio-visual presentation explained the story of the Battle of Athelstaneford and the birth of the St Andrew's saltire flag.

The functions of the now-defunct World Federation fell on the St Andrew Society. Affiliation to the St Andrew Society was regarded by many St Andrew and Caledonian societies as a mark of recognition. On St Andrew's Day, the society sent out greetings and a sprig of heather to all affiliates. The annual Newsletter was sent to all members and affiliates. Every year the St Andrew Society sent out information about St Andrew and the Athelstaneford vision to schools and this has raised the profile of St Andrew's Day.

On the principle that the groundwork had to be laid early, the St Andrew's Day competition run in schools by the society presented a number of awards for originality and variety in interpreting the meaning of St Andrew and his day. These consisted of plaques and saltire flags.

In 1994, for example, the main winner of the competition was Denny Primary School. There, all 250 pupils took part in a parade (headed by flag-bearers and all the boys who were called Andrew) from the school to a service at Denny Parish Church. Then it was back to school for an open day. During the afternoon the pupils performed a new dance called 'St Andrew of Denny,' which involved the pupils, dressed in their blue sweatshirts, forming four blue triangles of the saltire and others (dressed in white) dancing along the diagonals. Pupils also designed a new logo for the school and the winning design incorporated a saltire.

This was followed by a narration of the 'fishers of men' Gospel story told in the Scots tongue. Headteacher Miss Elizabeth Snaddon commented:

> I think it is important that the children know there is a patron saint and are aware that it is not just any other day. What we do does give the children enjoyment but the activities we do also covers every aspect of the curriculum. We want to make sure it is a special day for them.

The year before (1993) it was Parkside Primary School, Jedburgh which won. Headteacher Ken Fotheringham explained:

> Like many schools, we have a concert on St Andrew's Day and sing Scots songs with performances of a variety of kinds – the story of St Andrew in word and picture; Scottish games, Scottish dances and a play about Robert Louis Stevenson with poems. The programme naturally varies from year to year and we have outside adult performers and a piper. The children are given saltire stickers and shortbread.
>
> In 1993, we had a school competition with a 'Make a St Andrew's Day Card' challenge. Each class

won a prize for their best entry. A Primary Six class made up a questionnaire and asked people on 30 November in Jedburgh High Street if they knew it was St Andrew's Day? Would they send a St Andrew's Day card if such were available?

The response was mixed. Not everyone realised it was St Andrew's Day and not everyone promised to send cards! But it was a worthwhile exercise.

Another important organisation is the Saltire Society. Founded in 1936, the idea for the Saltire Society arose during a conversation between George Malcolm Thomson and Professor Andrew Dewar Gibb. The objects of the society are: to advance the education of the public by fostering and enriching the cultural heritage of Scotland in all its aspects, including the Scots and Gaelic languages; looking to the future as well as to the past and encouraging creativity in Scotland as a living element of European civilisation; being concerned with all aspects of Scottish life at home and abroad and by giving expression to the views of the society as necessary within the constraints that it has no party political or sectarian affiliation; co-operating with other institutions on matters, issues or undertakings which conform with the object of the society.

As well as publishing books under its own imprint, the Saltire Society adjudicates and administers a number of awards in the fields of history, architecture, civil engineering and planning, fine art, science, literature, education and Scots song.

The society strives to encourage anything that will improve the quality of life in Scotland and restore the country to its proper place as a creative force in European civilisation. The society also seeks to revive the memory of famous Scots and to make the nation conscious of its heritage.

In 2011, the St Andrew Society in Edinburgh took the decision to merge with the Saltire Society, so creating an admirable pooling of resources and a focusing of functions; a new combined body that would be stronger than they each were individually. The Scottish Flag Trust continues to run the Heritage Centre at Athelstaneford and its education and tourism function, as an independent body.

Societies Abroad

Perhaps the greatest concentration of St Andrew societies is to be found in the United States. In Charleston, South Carolina on 30

November 1729, the world's first society of St Andrew was formed. Founded by immigrant Scots, many from Aberdeen and Fife, it was dedicated to the relief of suffering and distress among inhabitants of the infant colony.

St Andrew's Feast Day is the prime event of the St Andrew's Society of North Carolina annual calendar, although it is never celebrated on 30 November. That date is too close to the national holiday of Thanksgiving, a time when families come together, usually for a Thursday to Sunday long weekend. As a practical matter, this society celebrates the Saint's Day on the Saturday following the Thanksgiving weekend. This is usually on a date in early December. For many, this constitutes the start of the Christmas season.

There is another small problem. Most members believe that 30 November is the birthday of the saint. They have to be reminded constantly that it is the Feast Day, established by the early church, and that the true birth date of the saint is unknown.

The society organises the annual St Andrew's Day Banquet which is open to all members and their guests. A prominent speaker with a strong Scottish background is the main feature, with a small pipe band as part of the entertainment. The programme might also have singers and dancers in place of a featured speaker. Attendance at these banquets runs to 160 or more. The dinners are held in a resort area central to the state of North Carolina. The program includes the 'Salute to the Haggis', 'Toasts to the Saint, the Queen and the President', and a 'Report from Brother Scots'.

Each year on or around 30 November, members of Fredericton Society of St Andrew (founded 1825) hold a St Andrew's dinner with friends and family. The program consists of a recital by the Fredericton Society of St Andrew Pipe Band. Following the conclusion of the pipes and drums entertainment, dinner is served at an appropriate time and the haggis is piped in. A pre-selected person recites the 'Address to the Haggis', and as the society has an excellent haggis-maker, guests and members are extremely complimentary. At a suitable moment the president introduces the speaker.

During the celebration of recent years there had been no reference to St Andrew. While there were no vociferous complaints about this sad omission, a few members expressed their dismay about this neglect of Scotland's patron saint. Members hoped that the society executive would 'get the message' and alert future speakers to inject a solid reference to St Andrew.

On the Sunday following the St Andrew's dinner, members attend

St Andrew's Presbyterian Church and participate in divine service led by the society chaplain. The society has both male and female members with a total membership of about 200. One of the earliest recipients of the society's charity was John Campbell whose case was considered in November 1826. Campbell was in distress and needed clothing. The society provided him with a pair of trousers, a shirt, a yard of broad cloth, a comforter, shoes, socks and a Scotch bonnet. In the 1860s a Scots widow appeared before the society for aid. She had three children, two being orphans of her sister's. One of the children was dying from consumption. She lived in very poor circumstances but was helped by the society and given eight dollars.

The first dinner of the society in 1826 seems to have been a gargantuan affair with 22 toasts! Unfortunately the bill of fare has not survived. The dinner began with a dirge in pious memory of St Andrew, followed by 'God Save the King'. The second dinner, a year later, is faithfully recorded in great detail. Among the meats available in the first course were boiled fowls, roast fowls, tongue, loin of veal, leg of mutton, haggis and boiled ham. The vegetables included mashed potatoes, turnips, boiled onions, beets, and carrots.

The second course offered mince pies, tarts, whips, apple pies, partridge, blancmange, ducks, plum pudding, goose and apple sauce! For the third course there were 'plenty of apples, raisins, nuts, olives, bread, butter and cheese, as well as celery left over from the second course.'

From Springfield, Missouri, Todd Wilkinson describes some of the reasons why St Andrew's societies are still being formed, the almost biological splitting and coalescence by which they are born and the networking skills employed to bring them to birth: 'The Scottish St. Andrew's Society of Springfield, Missouri, was formed on 24 June 2004 from former members of the Celtic Society of the Ozarks.[43] Through the assistance of Mr. Steve Grant, Sir James Grant (the Missouri Convener of the Clan Grant Society of the United States, Lord Strathspey and Chief of the Clan Grant), agreed to serve as the Society's honorary patron.'

At present the society has around 90 members on the rolls, comprised of Scottish expatriates and Americans of Scottish heritage. The mission of the society is to 'preserve and promote the Scottish and Scots-Irish heritage of Springfield and the Ozarks', although anyone interested in 'all things' Scottish may join the society, regardless of heritage.

The society celebrates St Andrew's Day with a church service on the first Saturday in November, since 30 November is between the

Thanksgiving and Christmas holidays. The service is traditionally held at St John's Episcopal Church, Springfield. The service also contains elements of a traditional Remembrance Day service, since Veteran's Day is celebrated on 11 November. The society gives the offering of the service to a local charity, in keeping with the original spirit of St Andrew's Societies around the world.

The society also holds its annual Robert Burns Supper in January, which is the largest event in its year, as well as a Kirkin' of the Tartans service in April and a Bannockburn Ball in June to celebrate the Scottish victory at Bannockburn, and the founding of the society. The society sponsors several other educational and social events throughout the year, and participates in the annual Missouri Tartan Day festivities and parade in April at St Charles, Missouri.

Started by a local history professor, the Celtic Society of the Ozarks was formed in 1986 and was a pan-Celtic organisation for Scots, Irish, Welsh, and people from and/or descended from the seven Celtic Nations. At the time, none of the different Celtic groups were large enough to form its own organisation, so they joined together and celebrated Burns Night, St Patrick's Day and St David's Day.

By 2000, the Scots became the predominant group, and in 2004, the decision was made for the Scots to form their own organization. Some of this was due to the fact that the word 'Celtic' denotes different things to different people – there were a lot of phone enquiries from people in the Pagan/Wiccan community who associated 'Celtic' with new age religion. So, it was decided to form a more traditional St Andrew's society, since it was more easily recognisable as a 'Scottish' organisation.

The St Andrew Society, Albuquerque, New Mexico has a membership of around 200 families. Their largest gathering is for the Robert Burns Night which is well attended by non-members. The St Andrew Night is celebrated with a Dinner or Pot-Luck Supper – pipers and drummers sometimes play on these occasions. Many years ago, members could look forward to a box of heather that the Scottish schoolchildren picked and packed and sent overseas to them. It was always a thrill to receive this gift, but the postage became so high that it had to be stopped.

In May each year Highland Games are held with herding dog demonstrations, rugby tournaments, Highland Dance and pipe and drum competitions. Traditionally, another British society, the Daughters of the British Empire, organise the tea tent for which they bake Scottish shortbread.

The St Andrew Scottish Society of New Mexico publishes a newsletter whose title is The Thistle Epistle. The cosmopolitan nature of ex-pat associations can be seen in the activities shared with other national societies – a Ceilidh with the Irish-American Society or a Pot-Luck supper at the German-American Club.

Organised in 1863, during the colourful days of California's Gold Rush, the St Andrew's Society of San Francisco was formed by a group of Scotsmen anxious to preserve and further their own traditions and culture and to aid Scots in distress. The society brought together those who longed to hear their own speech, the skirl of the bagpipe and the music and poetry of the Scotland they had left behind.

Today, aid to people of Scots origin or descent in distress remains an important function for the society, whose Board of Student Assistance, for example, helps students who are from Northern California or from Scotland.

In terms of cultural promotion, encouragement in tangible form is given to bagpipe bands, Highland dance groups and Celtic music study. The society's 'Hospitality Tent' is a feature of Highland Games held across Northern California.

The St Andrew's Society of the Eastern Shore is so named because most of its members reside on the eastern shore of Chesapeake Bay, an area comprising portions of three states – Delaware, Maryland and Virginia (the so-called DelMarVa Peninsula).

Membership is available to men and women of Scottish birth or ancestry. The society also provides charitable and educational assistance to Scottish men and women, their descendants and their widows or widowers.

To help promote and perpetuate Scottish traditions and culture, the society sponsors instruction in pipes, drums and Scottish country dancing. Its social activities include meetings, luncheons, dinners, picnics and ceilidhs. The society is not affiliated to any secular or religious organisation.

Every November, members celebrate the birth of St Andrew by sponsoring a dinner in his honour (during which their newly-elected officers and directors are installed). In the summer of 1995, for example, with the help of financial grants from the society, two young ladies from the area visited Scotland. One was participating in the 'People to People' programme; the other conducting an archaeological dig in north-west Scotland.

In the north-east of America, on 6 January 1657, only 20 years after the founding of the city, the Scots Charitable Society of Boston was organised for the relief of Scots. Almost a century later in 1749, the St Andrew's Society of Philadelphia was founded by 25 Scottish residents to give relief to the poor and the distressed. Two signatories of the Declaration of Independence – James Wilson (a graduate of St Andrews University) and John Witherspoon DD, a native of Paisley and president of Princeton College – were founder members.

Menu for the 166th annual banquet of the St Andrew's Society of Philadelphia at Bellevue, Stratford, on 30 November 1915.

Nearly ten years later, in 1756 the St Andrew's Society of the State of New York was founded as a charitable organisation. Colonel Simon Fraser, the eldest son of Lord Lovat, was a member. The society has a membership today of close to 1,000. The society holds an annual banquet at the Waldorf-Astoria hotel with two guest speakers on the topics 'The Land we live in' and 'The Land o' Cakes'. In 1994 the speaker on the latter theme was the late Lord Younger of Prestwick. The evening's entertainment is provided by two pipe bands, herald trumpeters, the singing of Scottish songs, and a haggis ceremony.

In 1994 the bill of fare consisted of cock-a-leekie soup; haggis, mashed turnips and oat cakes. This was followed by sirloin of beef, roast potatoes, glazed baby carrots and sautéed zucchini, finishing with shortbread and a choice of wine or whisky. Pipes and drums, the presentation of colours and Scots songs enlivened the proceedings. Present were representatives from many societies including the Sons of the American Revolution, the Society of Colonial Wars and Scottish Heritage USA, Inc.

The North British Society in Halifax, Nova Scotia was founded in 1768 and (outside Great Britain), is said to be the oldest Scottish heritage society in the Commonwealth, being open to persons of Scottish relationship by descent, marriage or affiliation. In its very first year, the founders 'unanimously agreed that the annual feast of this society be held on St Andrew's Day'. The founders' decision has been observed ever since, with certain particular exceptions – for instance, during the years of world wars.

The society's historian and past president, Donald F Maclean, writes:

> When we toast St Andrew we have a sense of honouring Scotland, our own Scottish antecedents and heritage. Perhaps we do not have quite so strong a sense of honouring a religious figure. St Andrew may have come to be, for us, primarily a symbol of patriotism. But our Nova Scotia flag, (the flag of Scotland with colours reversed), is a constant reminder, at least subconsciously, of St Andrew.

Nineteen years after the founding of Halifax (1749), and five years before the arrival of the ship *Hector* in 1773 which marked the beginning of mainstream Scottish emigration to Nova Scotia, a small group of Scots immigrants met in Halifax to organise the North British Society.

According to the literature of the society, use of the term 'Great Britain' instead of 'Scotland' was characteristic of the 18th-century enlightenment's ardent belief that eventually there would be achieved a common and vital *British* culture. In the 18th century the expression 'North Britain' did not imply any notion that Scotland was a secondary or subordinate adjunct to a larger power.

Poignantly aware that 'sickness and death are the common lot of all mankind', the group resolved to bind themselves into a society 'for the benefit of ourselves and assistance of each other, who may be afflicted with disease or any other casualty or misfortune'. Through the years, the society has extended financial assistance to persons and families in need, to destitute widows, to shipwrecked mariners, and worked for the return of elderly persons to their homes in Scotland.

Public gifts by the society have included a statue of Robert Burns, a bust of Sir Walter Scott, the Robert Stevenson Memorial Library and the presentation of microfiche copies of the surviving parish records (1553-1854) of the Church of Scotland. In more recent years, the society has also organised the Metropolitan Festival and Highland Games, a showcase for promoting the image and raison d'être of the society.

The St Andrew's Society of Washington honours St Andrew as part of their annual Kirkin' o' the Tartan at the National Cathedral each April. They also honour him in one of the toasts at the annual 'Burns Nicht' Dinner.

In his 'Toast to St Andrew', Jim MacGregor cleverly makes the connection between St Andrew and the character traditionally attributed to the Scot.

They say a Scot is thrifty. St Andrew lived with his brother and the family. Maybe he did so because he was single. On the other hand, maybe he was saving his pennies.

A Scot is thought to have an independent spirit – not bound by tradition. We know that Andrew was a follower of John the Baptist who preached against the establishment and its traditions. John was not a popular figure among the ruling class.

We Scots are said to have an open mind and to value learning. Andrew sought an interview with the Lord to hear the gospel message first-hand. He had to determine for himself whether or not to follow Him.

They say a Scot has enthusiasm and the courage of his convictions. Andrew believed the Lord. He went to his brother, Peter and told him he had found the Messiah. He introduced Peter to the Lord. Could it be said that St Andrew was the first domestic missionary?

We all know a Scot has reserve. Andrew was one of the first four Apostles. He is always mentioned with, but less frequently than, the other three. Maybe he was not part of the 'inner circle' – or perhaps he was and just did not blether about it.

'Scots are said to have a metaphysical bent. Andrew was one of those who inquired of the Lord about the signs of the end times.

A Scot is practical, a man of action. Andrew heard the discussion of how to feed the thousands of people. He found the boy with the five barley loaves and two fish. He directed the people to be seated. Maybe he also supervised the distribution.

A Scot can be a devoted, dutiful servant. The Greeks wanted an interview with the Lord. They asked Philip. Andrew took the request to the Lord. Could St Andrew have been the first missionary to foreigners?

A Scot is loyal. Andrew was with the others in the upper room in the scary time after the Lord's ascension. St Andrew is a true role model for us Scots!

Meeting of the St Andrew's Society of Baltimore during the Civil War.
(Courtesy of the St Andrew's Society of Baltimore)

Founded in 1806, St Andrew's Society of Baltimore takes part in an annual Kirkin' of the Tartans ceremony. With the Kiltie Band, about 35 men in Highland day-wear parade along the streets of Baltimore for four blocks before marching into church. During the service, which is dedicated to St Andrew, the tartans of the clans of Scotland are piped to the altar and blessed. After the congregation sings the 'Old Hundredth', the tartans are presented as the following prayer is recited:

> God of our fathers and mothers and of the long line of brave and good people who brought honour to Scotland by keeping the light of faith and patriotism in dark days, who surrounded hardships and sorrow with skirling pipes and the colours of unconquerable clans, and who celebrated life with dance and song and your gift of Highland dew; We, the descendants, now bring before you these tartans, symbols of our families past and present. We ask your blessing on them and all that they

stand for; that we, in our generation, may pass on to others the spiritual greatness that we have received, for the honour of your Name and for the well-being of all mankind. In the name of Andrew the Apostle and patron saint of Scotland, and of Jesus Christ our Lord.

Every year the society holds a banquet in honour of St Andrew attended by about 450 men. After grace, and toasts to the President of the United States and to Scotia, the haggis is addressed. Speeches are interwoven with piping and the music of the pipes and drums before the evening ends with the singing of 'Auld Lang Syne'.

First organised in 1803, the St Andrew's Society, Albany, New York has a membership today of around 100 men. Some of the more active, younger members are native Scots who have come over in the past decade. The work of the society is of a charitable nature.

Born out of concern and love for fellow countrymen on 8 February 1802, the society began as the United Irish and Scotch Benevolent Society. A year later, this group was dissolved and 18 men of Scottish birth (who had belonged to the original organisation) founded the St Andrew's Society at Tontines Coffee House on 7 October 1803.

The early days of the society were devoted to aiding the many immigrants from Scotland. Over the years, the society has given a considerable amount of money as gifts, grants and loans to individuals, charities, civic organisations and various Scottish causes.

Among the distinguished Scots who have been members are Joseph Henry, founder of the US national weather service, secretary of the Smithsonian Institution and discoverer of electrical magnetism. Another was the industrialist Andrew Carnegie.

The society meets five times a year at the Rooms, a historic three-storey building which includes a main meeting room, decorated with Clan shields, a baronial fireplace and many Scottish artefacts. Other features include a Wee Kitchen (based on the kitchen in the home of Robert Burns), an extensive library (established with a gift of Andrew Carnegie in 1902) and a large garden.

St Andrew's Day is the highlight of the society's year, with a dinner often consisting of Cameronian Haggis, Cock-a-Leekie Soup and Inverewe Salad, followed with a choice of Prime Ribs of Glaswegian Beef, Breast of Spey Valley Chicken or Broiled Aberdeen Salmon.
The haggis is presented, preceded by pipes and Armorer and recitation of Burns' 'To a Haggis'. Toasts are given to the President of the

United States, Her Majesty the Queen, Men and Women in Uniform and to the society. After the installation of the officers for the coming year, the members stand and sing 'Auld Lang Syne.'

Up to about 20 years ago the custom was to recite excerpts from Wallace Bruce's 'St Andrew's Sons':

> A miracle of truth divine,
> A martyr's cross, a hallowed shrine ...
> The martyr's lips at Patras stilled,
> The Scottish heart with triumph thrilled.

In 2010 the society established the Robert Tunnicliffe Heritage Foundation to promote Scottish culture by awarding grants to students who are involved in Scottish arts.

Founded in 1923, the object of the St Andrew's Society of Rhode Island is to foster interest in and to promote the study of Scottish folklore, history, literature and tradition by providing opportunities for the presentation and discussion of subjects of interest to its members; to promote social activities and to support charitable enterprises as financially feasible and to further any desirable or deserving Scottish movement as so directed by the officers and executive committee.

The society holds its St Andrew's Day celebration in mid-November to avoid conflict with Thanksgiving (the last Thursday in November). There is a 'Kirking of the Tartans' on the Sunday closest to Veterans Day (11 November). One member writes that, 'We always place a wee bit of tartan ribbon on the church program so that we can take it and stick it in on one's clothing and become Scottish for an hour or so'.

The following Saturday a dinner dance is held, buffet-style complete with the Haggis Ceremony, Scottish music and country dancing. Some members are also vendors of Scottish goods and apparel. They take annual turns to display their wares and ten percent of the profit is donated to the St Andrew's Society of Rhode Island Scholarship Fund, Inc.

Membership of the society is made up not only of adult men and women but also of children and grandchildren, for whom there is a children's storytelling party at a date after the dinner dance and before Thanksgiving. The service itself includes a reading of the Psalm 23 in Scots:

The Laird's my Herd, I sallnae want;
He loots me to lie doon,
At owre the knowes, an' in green howes,
Whaur bonnie burnies croon.
My saul He waukins frae its dwam,
Oot o' the muirlands weet,
Intil richt roads – for His Name's sake –
He airts my wann'ring feet.
Na, to' I hae to gang my lane,
Doon through the deid mirk dale,
I'll thole nae skaith, for ye are bye,
Your crook an' kent ne'er fail.
My grainin' buird ye've hanselit, while
My faes did sit an' glower;
My pow wi' Ile is dreepin wat,
My bicker's lippin ower.
Guid guidin' an' guid greenin' sall
Gang wi' me late an' air;
An' syne up i' the Laird's big hoose
I'll bide for ever mair.

According to one of the programmes of the society, The 'Kirking of the Tartans' recalls that 'for Highland clansmen, the tartan signified a covenantal relationship between God and each family of believers'. It is also a 'remembrance of the Patron Saint of Scotland and a celebration of heritage and a rededication to the service of God'.

In Canada, the St Andrew's Society of Montreal was established in 1835, setting up the St Andrew's Home and other directly charitable agencies. The St Andrew's Society of Toronto followed a year later. The London, Ontario St Andrew's and Caledonian Society appeared around 1875.

As one contemporary publication put it: 'By most of these societies the 30th day of November in each year is observed as a time of great rejoicing. Then the patriot-

Past president of the St Andrew's Society of Montreal, Alexander McGibbon, merchant and inspector in the Department of Indian Affairs; b.13 Feb 1829 in Petite-Côte (Montreal) d.24 Feb 1904 in Calgary. (Courtesy of the St Andrew's Society of Montreal, Canada)

ism of the members is freely expressed, and they extol their native land, its hills and valleys and streams, its men and women, its history, its battles, its antiquities, its discoveries'.

Founded in 1835, the principal aims of the St Andrew's Society of Montreal are to sustain, assist and encourage those less fortunate kith of Scottish birth or descent; to provide youth of Scottish ancestry in the Province of Quebec with opportunities to advance their education through bursaries, scholarships and loans; to maintain and preserve Scottish traditions in the community by promoting historical, cultural, patriotic, social and sporting activities.

The first Scots to celebrate St Andrew's Day in Montreal may have been those who served with the Chevalier Johnstone in the army of Louis X. The Scots fighting for George III certainly did so.

The first recorded St Andrew's Ball was held on 2 December 1816. The *Montreal Herald* describes the scene:

> The dancing commenced about seven o'clock and continued with great spirit till after midnight, when the company to the number of about 130, sat down to a sumptuous and elegant supper ... The supper room was handsomely decorated, having at the upper end a transparency of glass lit behind by candles representing St Andrew at full length.
>
> Suppers were lavish: a pyramid of quail, a suckling pig à l'Italienne and a boar's head. The entry of the haggis was a central feature. After supper the dancing continued with much vivacity till five o'clock.

In its earliest years the primary function of the society was to administer charity from funds collected. In 1852, for example, travel expenses of £94 were provided to Scots immigrants; some £372 was paid to the families of those killed in the Crimean War and £263 transferred to local charities.

The first of a series of St Andrew's Homes for the accommodation of immigrants was rented in 1857. When a disastrous fire broke out on the SS *Montreal* (320 of whose passengers were Scots immigrants), some 254 people were killed. Around 76 of the survivors were cared for in the society's new St Andrew's Home. The Committee arranged for the identification and burial of the dead, and the disposition of their clothing and personal belongings. In the pocket of one of the victims was found a stanza of 'The Exile's Song':

Oh! Why left I my hame,
Why did I cross the deep?
Oh! Why left I the land
Where my forfathers sleep?
I sigh for Scotia's shore,
And I gaze across the sea:
But I canna get a blink
O' my ain countrie!

Since its inception, the society has taken pride in its members as builders of Canada. In 1858, a bill was enacted to broaden the powers of the society, enabling it to carry out welfare and youth-training activities among those of Scottish birth or descent, as well as social, artistic and sporting activities to preserve Scottish traditions. In 1972, over $17,000 was spent on welfare and education grants.

Moving further east, across the Pacific Ocean, Singapore St Andrew's Society founded around 1836, celebrates St Andrew's Day with an annual ball for around 400 guests. In addition to flying in a guest speaker, the society provides a Scottish band (for many years the Neil Barron Scottish Country Dance band) and a piper. Normally there is an exhibition dance by the society's Country Dance team, along with performances by the Gurkha Contingent of the Singapore Police Force. Atholl Brose is served before dinner.

In 1994 the society's dinner consisted of cock-a-leekie soup; haggis, turnip and potatoes, Scottish salmon, a sweet (Blairgowrie Delight) with cheese and oatcakes.

Members of the society like to welcome guests from other countries, such as surprised and delighted Australians Ross and Kathy Taylor who gave a personal reaction to the ceremonies in the society's newsletter:

'OK, yeah sure we'd like to come,' was our innocent response to the invitation to go to the 1994 St Andrew's Ball. Before we knew it we were being embroiled in all types of odd Scottish traditions. Whoever heard of a Ball that you practise for? We didn't think they could possibly be serious.

In no time, we were having explained to us what sets, pousettes and strathspeys were. We had always thought a strathspey was an Aussie cat, but you live and learn. We were then asked to put these strange terms into practice, while simultaneously trying to remember the actual dance sequence, keep in time with the music and concentrate on the different instructions that seemed to be flooding in from all directions.

To our surprise, however, over the six weeks prior to the Ball, we found ourselves making tangible progress and actually enjoying ourselves.

By the time the night of the Ball was upon us, we found ourselves regretting we weren't Scottish with a long history of dancing, kilt-wearing and bagpipe-blowing.

When you get inside the main reception room at the Shangri-la Hotel you find it's as if you have been beamed up out of Singapore to somewhere in the Scottish Highlands. It seemed that tartan and kilts were taking over the world.

In the ballroom we learnt our first Scottish phrase: 'Lang may yer lum reek! – ye cowrin' timrous beastie.'

The bagpipes started to honour the entry of the haggis. Who would have thought someone would fly a bag of entrails half way around the world, honour its entry to a Ball with bagpipes, drums and 600 people standing, arrange for it to be greeted ceremoniously by a Chieftain and finally have it served up with silver service and laced with 12-year old Scotch whisky?

Moving closer to Scotland, the Belfast Benevolent Society of St Andrew has been in continuous operation since its foundation in 1867 and members have held a St Andrew's Day Dinner each year, with the exception of two years during the First World War. In November 1810, the following appeared in the Belfast Newsletter:

The Festival of St Andrew, the Tutelar Saint of Scotland, will be celebrated at the Donegall Arms on Friday, 30 November 1810. Dinner on the table at five o'clock. The stewards give this general invitation to all Scotch Gentlemen who may find it convenient to attend and they require the honour of the Company of such Irish Gentlemen as incline to be of the party. Tickets three crowns each.

The society was founded through the efforts of David Taylor of Perth and John Arnott from Auchtermuchty who had arrived in Belfast in the early 1860s. Together they founded Arnott's Stores. John Arnott later became Mayor of Cork and David Taylor was elected Mayor of Belfast. Both were subsequently knighted.

The aims of the society, were to alleviate distress among Scots and their dependants; to assist charitable objectives and to afford opportunity for social meetings. However, it was hoped that the new society 'would be the means of bringing together in closer communion Scots who, while cherishing a lively regard for the country they live in, are yet desirous of showing they do not forget the land which gave them birth.' There was a caveat: 'It is not, however, a society for the encouragement of mutual esteem, or for the fostering of that sort of nationalism which loves to dwell on the meaner and provincial attributes of a country, or at best to elevate it to the comparative detriment of another.'

The St Andrew's Society of Kobe, Japan holds a spring and an autumn ceilidh. Members also have a Burns Supper and a St Andrew's Ball. The society's annual general meeting is held in April, usually followed by another ceilidh. The ceilidhs normally attract about 50 people, both Scottish and Japanese. Normally about 100 members and guests attend the ball. The society is open to all comers, but the committee members must have Scottish blood.

In Africa, the Harare Caledonian Society of Zimbabwe usually celebrated St Andrew's Day annually with a dinner dance. The emphasis in the evening was on St Andrew. During the course of the night two speakers were invited to address the gathering. The main topic has been 'St Andrew and Bonnie Scotland', the speaker being invited to discourse for about 15 minutes, after which those present were asked to drink a toast to St Andrew. The second speaker's topic was usually 'The Land we live in'.

The St Andrew Society of Rio de Janeiro was founded in 1906 by a group of Scottish businessmen intent on supporting local charities by organising social events of a Scottish nature for the enjoyment of the local community at large. In 1994 the society was holding on to its core values and in the midst of a worldwide economic depression, had record attendances at events to celebrate the 250th anniversary of the birth of Scotland's national bard, Robert Burns. This was due largely to a group of long-term Scottish residents in Macaé who worked offshore.

Traditional events were spaced out over the year: a Robert Burns celebration, sprinkled with local wit, a golf competition between the society and the Macaé oilmen, followed by a ceilidh. The Caledonian Ball was held in the magnificent ballroom of the Copacabana Palace Hotel with the Iain MacPhail Scottish Country Dance Band from Edinburgh. The Macaé Ceilidh was held at the Sheraton Hotel in Macaé, again with the Iain MacPhail Scottish Country Dance Band. Every Tuesday from April till October there was Scottish country dancing. By 2013, however, the black-tie dinner for St Andrew's Day which had been 'men only' until 1960, was no more. A few years ago there was a boat trip, but recently there has been no event around November 30 due to lack of interest.

Further down South America, the St Andrew's Society of the River Plate, Buenos Aires, Argentina is a flourishing one. On the nearest Sunday to 30 November members celebrate a St Andrew's Day Service at the St Andrew's Presbyterian City Church with the attendance of staff from the British Embassy and other special guests. The Pipe Band of the society plays at the service.

On the Saturday before the service, members organise a St Andrew's Day banquet held at the English Club. There, beside the performance of the Pipe Band and Highland Dancers, members parade with the banners of the clans of individual members of the society, eat haggis and dance Scottish country dances with great abandon.

Still in South America, the St Andrew's Society of Uruguay (founded 1895) annually celebrates St Andrew's Day at the residence of the British Ambassador with a dinner to which guests are invited to attend in highland dress, dinner jackets or dark suits. Normally there are over 80 persons present to enjoy the four-course dinner (including haggis – which is brought in ceremoniously accompanied by two pipers). Speeches are followed by toasts to 'The Land in which we live', 'Bonnie Scotland', 'The Lassies' and a 'Reply from the Lassies'. After dinner there is the ever-popular Scottish dancing. Former President Martin Fraser Gibson comments that, 'St Andrew as the Patron Saint of Scotland, is part of our Scottish heritage and is the instigator of all our Scottish traditions and events'.

In Australia, the multiplicity of Scottish societies and the eventual need to amalgamate them into a larger organisation is most evident in Victoria to where many Scots emigrated in the early 1800s and formed the Victorian Scottish Union. Poverty, famine and epidemics in Scotland in the 1820s and 1830s caused the first significant Scottish emigration to Australia, with Victoria the most popular colony in which to settle. Scottish squatters and rural workers established farms, and urban settlers worked as skilled artisans and professionals. For example, the first immigrant ship to arrive in Port Phillip, on 27 October 1839, was the *David Clark* from Greenock. In the first Victorian census of 1854, Scottish-born people were the third largest group after the English and Irish-born, with 36,044 people. Within three years a further 17,000 had arrived, many hoping to make their fortunes on the goldfields. In 1856, Geelong's *Commun Na Fienne* was formed, followed by Maryborough Highland Society the following year. A year later the Ballarat Caledonian Society and the Royal Caledonian Society of Victoria (now Melbourne) were established; Bendigo followed suit in 1859 by also forming a Caledonian Society, all still very active today.

Meeting of the Victorian Scottish Union, 9 Sept 1908.
(Courtesy of the VSU)

The first meeting of the Victorian Scottish Union took place on 20 September 1906, when delegates from the affiliated societies assembled at the Shire Hall in Rushworth.[44] Since the idea of a union was floated new societies had sprung up, increasing the total from 15 to 50 societies. Around 40 delegates arrived by the midday train from all parts of Australia. A strong representation from the local society assembled at the railway station and gave the delegates a warm welcome, afterwards escorting them to the Criterion Hotel, the procession headed by 'the wee M'Gregor' playing the pipes. After dinner the business meeting was held, prior to which the delegates were photographed in front of the Hall.[45]

The Melbourne Scots were founded in 1919. The society is open to men of Scottish birth or descent but has a 'no publicity' rule and functions are communicated only to members. 'We have found this policy to operate well', writes the then honorary secretary, John G Cooper, 'especially as many of our members and guests are "newsworthy". We therefore offer them freedom from Press photography and reporting when they attend activities of the Society'. Membership is limited to 240 and, as vacancies arise, they are filled from the waiting list. Currently it takes around four years between going on the waiting list and admission.

The main activity of the society is a formal dinner. The society has a strong Banffshire/Aberdeenshire contingent within the membership and appreciates 'the Doric' language in the dinner menu – 'Haggis an' Atholl Brose; Hoch o' Hoggie wi' a jilp o' mushroom bree followed by Crumlie Kebbuck'.

The grace before dinner sums up the ethos of the society: 'For a goodly heritage, for proud traditions and cherished memories, for good fellowship and good fare, we give Thee thanks, O Lord and crave Thy blessing'.

The original members of the Napier NZ Scottish Society 1890. (Courtesy of the City of Napier Caledonian Society)

Moving across the Pacific again to New Zealand, the City of Napier Caledonian Society normally celebrates St Andrew's Day on the Sunday nearest the 30 November. The Pipe Band and the Scottish Country Dancers combine for a 'Kirkin' of the Tartan' at St Paul's Presbyterian Church. This is preceded by a formal march to the church with tartan banners proudly displayed. During the service, everyone present is invited to present their own tartan for blessing. The readings are given by representatives of Scottish organisations.

The second event on the 30 November, is a ceilidh involving all Scottish organisations – Scottish societies, pipe bands, Highland dancers and Scottish country dancers in the district. Although many members are third- and even fourth-generation New Zealanders, they greatly value their links with Scotland (the land of their forebears) and honour its Patron Saint. Members feel however that, to many people, St Andrew is just a name. This omission the society intends to redress. Typical of the depth of feeling experienced by members was the sermon delivered by the Revd Colin English on 29 November 1992 at St Paul's Presbyterian Church, Napier:

> Nationalism, pride in our nation, in one's social and cultural roots, in one's religious roots, is something to be welcomed when it enhances and enriches the life of the human family and our national family. Martin Niemoller is a potent reminder of the fallacy of compartmentalizing our lives on the basis of our own self-identi-

ty. Equally, distinctions can enrich and enhance the life of any community when we allow them. Nationalism and pride in our race and culture is good when it unites and bad when it divides. It is good when it gives me pride in my background and helps me to appreciate the background of others. It is bad, even idolatrous, when it cuts me off from others because they are 'different' from me, whether in religion, race or creed. It is bad when I feel no responsibility for others because they are identified by a label different from my own.

Further north, on the south coast of China, the Hong Kong St Andrew's Society celebrates St Andrew's Day with a St Andrew's Ball attended by some 600 people, including guests from the St George, St David and St Patrick societies. At the ball a toast is given to St Andrew, with reference to his biblical origins. It is an opportunity to gather together as Scots and celebrate all that is best in Scottish tradition and culture.

As well as a church service, there is a competition at a horse race meeting for the St Andrew's Quaich; the St Andrew's team also competes against the St George's team at rugby and there is a wreath-laying ceremony at which respects are paid to compatriots who lost their lives in battle.

The Selangor (Kuala Lumpur) St Andrew's Society was established in 1887 and has around 100 members, only half to three-quarters of whom were born or brought up in Scotland. Other members are of Scottish descent. The major social event of the year is the annual ball to which members can bring guests. During the first half of the evening, after the speeches and toasts, almost everyone takes part in the Scottish dancing which has been religiously practised by members and guests alike for weeks beforehand.

A programme note on the annual celebration menu-card records that St Andrew apparently first brought Christianity to Romania, where superstition has it that ghosts and werewolves roam the countryside on St Andrew's Day. 'Last year [1993]', continues the note, 'in Romania, a rural publication, *Evenimentul Zilei*, urged Romanians to consume large quantities of garlic and to rub it on the windows and doors of their homes to ward off werewolves, vampires and other malevolent spirits on St Andrew's Day'.

In 1994, beginning with the 'Selkirk Grace', the meal consisted of Scotch salmon rose, garnished with assorted lettuce and asparagus bouquet accompanied by balsamic vinaigrette. This was followed by haggis, neeps and tatties; *lamb persillade à l'Écosse* with rosemary sauce, served with carrot flan; a spiced flummery and Boh coffee or Boh tea. For the occasion the room was decorated with white heather, flags, banners, Bruce and Wallace shields, and a ram's head. When dancing commenced, the company was further enlivened with eight-some reels, a piping display, the 'Dashing White Sergeant' and 'Strip the Willow'.

* * *

Turning to Europe and Scandinavia, meanwhile, a unique and hon-ourable history is attached to the Caledonian Society of Norway (patron, the Duke of Argyll). During the period immediately follow-ing the Second World War, when a wave of spontaneous rejoicing flooded over Norway, many Allied soldiers took an active and very welcome part in Norwegian social life. Among them was Sergeant-Major James W Blair. On the evening of his arrival in Oslo, Sergeant-Major Blair went for a stroll up the hill in the direction of the royal palace. There he encountered a Norwegian, who was on his way down the hill towards the main street of Oslo, Karl Johan, a popular meet-ing place at that time of public rejoicing. The Norwegian was Willy Sommerfeldt Jacobsen. He and the Scottish soldier soon got into con-versation. This was the casual beginning to what would later develop into a warm friendship and mutual respect.

One day, Blair suggested to Sommerfeldt that they should start a Scottish-Norwegian society. By this time the Scot had made a large number of Norwegian friends.

On Wednesday 11 September 1946, Blair invited two fellow Scots and three Norwegians to his room at the Hotel Continental (No. 862), which was at that time reserved for Allied forces. Then he put to them his idea of forming a Scottish-Norwegian society. A tempo-rary committee was established and given the task of drawing up a constitution and enrolling members. On the committee was J Solheim, then a journalist on the *Morgenbladet*. He had previously been in contact with Blair when preparing an article on the Scots. He became the founder member and first secretary.

Blair was recalled to Scotland in the autumn of 1946, leaving Norway for good. However, the seed had been sown and by the fol-lowing year there were 16 members of the new Caledonian Society of Norway. The aim of the society was to form a cultural and intimate relationship between the two nations. Although this rather ambitious goal has not yet been fully met, the society has been a valuable link in the chain binding the Scotland and Norway together.

The two major functions in the society's year were St Andrew's Night and Burns' Night. At the monthly meetings in the Villa Granberg, lectures, films and other entertainment were regularly provided. In later years, meetings were held in Rune's Skipperstue or at Det norske Medicinske Selskab. A St Andrew's Night Ball was always a popular feature. In the dark November evenings guests were welcomed to it with flaring torches. They walked up the steps of the Villa Granberg on a red carpet, to be met by cheerful trumpet fanfares.

Dress at the ball (now, sadly, due to rising costs, no longer an annual event) was full Highland Dress or white tie, with ladies in all their finery. Sometimes a pantomime, based on historical events preceded dinner. These have included the story of King James VI of Scotland with his bride, Princess Anne of Norway.

After cocktails and dinner, the Grand March and ball began. On several occasions a piper was brought in from Scotland or from a Scottish regiment serving in Germany. Eightsome reels are always danced and the evening ended with 'Auld Lang Syne'.

Wreaths were also placed by the society at the unveiling of the monument commemorating British servicemen who fell in Norway during the Second World War.

Throughout important phases of Scandinavian history, Scots soldiers played a part. During the Kalmar War (1611-3) between Sweden and Denmark/Norway, 300 Scottish mercenaries were engaged by the Swedish King Charles IX and placed under the command of Lieutenant Colonel Alexander Ramsay. They were ordered to fight their way through Norway to join the king in Sweden.

The Scots landed at Romsdalsfjorden on 21 August 1612 and began to march up the valleys. However, at Kringen, local farmers assembled to prevent them passing. The farmers prepared an avalanche of wood and boulders and when a company led by Captain George Sinclair passed on the morning of 26 August, the avalanche was released, the Scots coming under heavy fire. Many died. The Norwegians took 134 prisoners, of whom only 18 survived. During the Second World War, around 50 British soldiers were killed in the same area. On 26 August 1962, some 12,000 people assembled to commemorate these events.

In 1981 the society was also instrumental in forming the Oslo Scottish Country Dancing Group, affiliated to the Royal Scottish

Country Dance Society. The Caledonian Society also provided tickets for members wishing to attend international football matches between Scotland and Norway at the Ulleval Stadion. At these matches, the society's pipe led the Scots team onto the field.

12
St Andrew and Modern Scotland

Public Holiday

The move to declare 30 November a public holiday dates back at least to 1907 with the foundation of the St Andrew's Society in Edinburgh, one of whose constitutional objectives was to encourage the celebration of 30 November as Scotland's national day. The society re-launched its campaign in 1987, gathering support from the Church of Scotland and the Roman Catholic Church, from the Scottish Trade Union Council, from individual trade unions and a number of political parties. Helen Liddell, at that time Scottish Secretary of the Labour Party, declared that 'the feeling of the Scottish Executive Committee was that St Andrew's Day should be a public holiday provided it was seen as an additional holiday' but the campaign was ignored by the Conservative government.

Today there are increasing numbers who are convinced of the need to declare St Andrew's Day a public holiday. In the early 1990s City of Edinburgh District Councillor Devin Scobie (Scottish Liberal Democrat Recreation and Tourism spokesman) waged a personal campaign in favour of a public holiday in Scotland on St Andrew's Day, saying that:

> Scotland has fewer recognised public holidays than the rest of the United Kingdom. We have none which mark or remember any part of our history or culture.
>
> Conversely, many towns and cities in Scotland have a bewildering variety of local and business holidays which few people really understand. If the Secretary of State does not support a St Andrew's Day Holiday, I would like to see the City of Edinburgh take the lead and replace one of its Spring local holidays with a St Andrew's Day holiday, perhaps on the Monday closest to 30 November. Our Patron Saint has gone without recognition for centuries. As we approach the new mil-

lennium, I would like to see the year 2000 as a target date for the new St Andrew's Day Holiday to be in place.

Of the Scottish MPs contacted by Councillor Scobie on 15 July 1994, some 26 were in favour of making 30 November a public holiday; nine were opposed to the idea and six refused to express an opinion. The number of Scottish MPs who favoured the proposal were: Labour (20 out of 47); Conservative (9 out of 10); Liberal Democrat (8 out of 9); Scottish National Party (3 out of 3).

The SNP's Andrew Welsh MP tabled an Early Day motion in the House of Commons on 29 November 1994 calling for the adoption of St Andrew's Day as a public holiday in Scotland. He commented that:

> It is an anomaly that the day celebrating Scotland's Patron Saint is not a public holiday in Scotland. Throughout Europe other countries have the day of their Patron Saint as an official public holiday. In comparison, Scotland has less public holidays than these other European countries. It is now time for the Government to make St Andrew's Day an official public holiday and to mark the day by encouraging the flying of the cross of St Andrew.

On 21 July 1995, Robert Maclennan (then MP for Caithness and Sutherland) responding to Councillor Scobie, tabled a Parliamentary Question to the then Secretary of State for Scotland, asking, 'If he will consider the designation of St Andrew's Day as a public holiday in Scotland'.

Replying in a written answer on behalf of the Secretary of State for Scotland, Lord James Douglas-Hamilton said: 'Public holidays in Scotland are not defined in statute, but by long tradition and practice are determined by individual local authorities in consultation with local interests. My Right Honourable Friend has no power to intervene in this process'.

In a letter to Robert Maclennan on 30 November 1994, Lord Fraser of Carmyllie QC , Minister for Home Affairs and Health, pointed out that, 'It is open to any authority to declare St Andrew's Day as a holiday; that none has apparently done so suggests that a holiday at the end of November may not be particularly attractive to many people.' He concluded that:

The Secretary of State has no power to intervene in the process of determining local public holidays and, given the limited significance of bank holidays in Scotland generally and the lack of public interest, the Government see no need to designate an additional Bank Holiday for St Andrew's Day.

It is, however, quite clear that the Secretary of State would have the power to designate St Andrew's Day a bank holiday. Paragraph 2 of Schedule 1 of the Banking and Financial Dealing Act 1971 designated the following days as Bank Holidays in Scotland-New Year's Day (if it be not a Sunday), or (if it be a Sunday) 3rd January; 2nd January (if it be not a Sunday); or (if it be a Sunday) 3rd January; Good Friday; the first Monday in May; the first Monday in August.

Section 1(92) of the Act gives the Queen the power to change the days set out in Schedule 1 by Royal Proclamation; and Section 1(93) gives her the power to appoint any other days as a Bank Holiday by Royal Proclamation.

There appears to be no reason why the Secretary of State for Scotland could not ask the Queen to declare St Andrew's Day (30 November) a Bank Holiday, by Royal Proclamation under Section 1 (93) of the Act. It might be that people in some places in Scotland would continue to treat it as a normal working day, but other might treat it as a public holiday.

Writing in *The Herald* on 1 December 1994, the Scottish National Party's Alex Salmond argued forcefully for a public holiday on 30 November:

> While other countries celebrate their national day in style, St Andrew is relegated to B-league status in his adopted homeland. Compared to the two other Scottish festivals – Burns Night and Hogmanay – the feast day of Andrew hardly gets a look in. I'm in favour of a national holiday for St Andrew's Day and the full works in terms of school projects, national competitions, sporting and cultural events. A proper remembrance of St Andrew would give us all the opportunity to reflect on

our national shortage of self worth and help give us the determination to change things for the better.

In an article published in *Flourish*, the newspaper of the Roman Catholic Archdiocese of Glasgow, Mr Salmond added that:

> Andrew the man knew the importance of hard work and the importance of working as a team for mutual benefit. He was a working fisherman, without education, but still chosen to provide leadership at a critical moment. He could still be an inspirational figure to the country which had the privilege of adopting his cross. A public holiday on St Andrew's Day could be an effective way of remembering some lessons about the simplicity of our roots and making some private vows about the need to work together to build a country more worthy of its Patron Saint.

Perceptively, novelist and commentator Allan Massie observed in *Scotland on Sunday* (27 November 1994) that, ' ... the first significance of Scotland's adoption of St Andrew as Patron Saint was that it put us at the heart of Europe'.

A *Scotland on Sunday* poll taken in 1995 found that only 39% knew the date of St Andrew's Day. At its annual general meeting that year – in response to the Tory Government's White Paper, 'Taking Stock' – the St Andrew's Society passed a resolution which included the request that 30 November should be a public holiday in Scotland. This was again ignored by the Conservatives. The civil servant who responded claimed that the Secretary of State had no power to intervene in the process of determining local holidays and that it was a matter for individual local authorities, most of whom preferred the traditional spring or autumn holidays at a time when the weather was better than in November.

The pressure continued. In March 2000, MSP Keith Raffan (Lib Dem) put forward a motion in the Scottish Parliament calling for a national public holiday on 30 November. However, *The Herald* reported that ministers planned to turn down any plea to make St Andrew's Day a public holiday. A Scottish Executive spokesperson added that, 'We have too many public holidays as it is.'

Undaunted, that October, the St Andrew's Society sent questionnaires to all Scottish Councils regarding St Andrew's Day. The results showed that fewer councils had a holiday on St Andrew's Day than prior to the local government reorganisation of 1996. Only Angus Council still had a holiday on 30 November. Previously, Councils such as Clackmannan, Clydesdale and Sutherland kept a public holiday, while Dumfries and Galloway celebrated with a school holiday. Few councils had expressed a view as to whether there should be a holiday, although Glasgow council's policy (following a 1998 resolution) was that there should be a holiday.

By December 2000 there was another Lib Dem motion (this time tabled by Iain Smith) calling for a St Andrew's holiday. In April 2001 it was reported in *The Sunday Times* (Scotland) that Trade Secretary Stephen Byres was actively considering the introduction of an extra bank holiday across the UK and that this was likely to be St Andrew's Day in Scotland.

October 2001 saw the press launch of the Scotsman of the Year Awards, to be presented on St Andrew's Day as a way of raising the profile of that day. Based in part on a similar initiative in Australia, the moving-force behind this event was Scots rugby star and national hero Gavin Hastings. Reports in *The Scotsman* had Labour First Minister Henry McLeish admitting that 'we can and should do much more to maximise the potential of St Andrew's Day, not only to promote our nation's heritage but also to promote Scotland today'. This sentiment was backed by the national tourism body, VisitScotland. There was a growing belief that St Andrew's Day for the Scots could and should imitate what St Patrick's Day did for the Irish.

Such enthusiasm and speculation was followed in September 2001 by a Department of Trade and Industry denial of this and similar press reports, adding that there were no plans to introduce an extra holiday to England and Wales and, furthermore, that it would not be consulting the business community on this. It was confirmed, nevertheless, that the question of Scottish bank holidays was the responsibility of the Scottish Executive.

This did little to dampen interest in the matter in the public domain, but there were also conflicting signals: a November 2001 opinion poll conducted by Famous Grouse whisky found that only 22% of people questioned knew that St Andrew's Day was on 30 November and 5% did not know the name of Scotland's patron saint. By contrast, a poll by whisky blenders Whyte & Mackay found that 68% of people wanted a national holiday on St Andrew's Day.

In the Scottish Parliament the result was that on 29 November, First Minister Jack McConnell (2001-2007) was asked by independent MSP Dennis Canavan:

> Given that a recent poll indicated that only two per cent
> of Scots know that tomorrow is St Andrew's Day, will
> the Scottish Executive make an effort to give Scotland a
> higher profile internationally as well as nationally by
> declaring St Andrew's Day a national holiday?

Replying, the First Minister said that he had tested opinion in
Wishaw and 'there seemed to be a general feeling that public holidays
in Scotland at this time of the year were not necessarily the best idea'.
He went on to say that, 'the debate is interesting and I am sure it will
go on, but I think that we have a job to do in using St Andrew's Day
to raise Scotland's profile internationally. We also have a job to do in
raising the profile of St Andrew's Day within Scotland'.

Over the next four years, Mr Canavan persisted. He planned to
bring a bill before the Scottish Parliament to have St Andrew's Day
made a bank holiday in Scotland. He carried out a consultation
across a wide spectrum of bodies and individuals in Scotland. This
revealed a substantial level of support, which would be essential for
the Bill to have a chance of being accepted for a First Reading in the
Scottish Parliament.

The St Andrew's Day Bank Holiday (Scotland) Bill, a Member's
Bill, was introduced by Dennis Canavan on 19 May 2005. The move
to make 30 November Scotland's national public holiday was backed
by 75 MSPs, including the Scottish Nationalists, the Scottish
Socialists, the Greens, 19 Labour and nine Liberal Democrat back-
benchers and some Tories (who stated that provided it did not add to
the total number of holidays, they would support it).

The bill went for Stage 1 debate on 6 October 2005. However,
First Minister Jack McConnell said he was not convinced by Dennis
Canavan's move, the main objections appearing to be the cost implications of another holiday. Therefore, the proposal was referred back
to the lead committee (the Enterprise and Culture Committee) for
further discussion. This amendment by the executive was narrowly
passed by 66 votes to 58, with no abstentions.

Writing early in the New Year 2006 to the author, MSP Dennis
Canavan outlined the progress of his Bill to date:

> My Bill to make St Andrew's Day a National Holiday
> initially attracted the support of 76 Members of the
> Scottish Parliament. A MORI opinion poll showed that
> 75 per cent of the people of Scotland support a St

Andrew's Day National Holiday and the nationwide consultation on my Bill indicated a similar level of support. The Enterprise & Culture Committee of the Scottish Parliament unanimously approved the general principles of the Bill.

During the public consultation, the Scottish Executive was conspicuous by its silence. However, at the eleventh hour, just before the Bill was debated in plenary session of the Parliament, the Executive lodged an amendment to refer the Bill back to the Committee. The Executive party bosses whipped their members to support the amendment which was passed by 66 votes to 58. It was an unprecedented piece of parliamentary skulduggery.

As a result, the Bill is now being re-considered by Members of the Enterprise & Culture Committee who will compile another report for further consideration by the Parliament. Contrary to some media reports, the Bill has not been killed off. I intend using every means at my disposal to keep it alive and to ensure that it becomes an Act of the Scottish Parliament.

Scotland is one of the few countries in the world which does not have a National Day holiday. It is also at the bottom of the European League in terms of the number of public holidays compared with our E[uro]pean] U[nion] partners. A St Andrew's Day National Holiday would give Scots the opportunity to celebrate our Patron Saint, our national identity and our cultural diversity. It would also help to promote Scotland throughout the world and recognise our membership of the international community.

While there can be no doubt about the historical importance of St Andrew as a symbol of Scottish identity, the logical step of declaring 30 November a public or a bank holiday was not universally accepted as desirable, specifically by the then senior politician in the Scottish Executive, First Minister Jack McConnell.

In April 2006, the Scottish Executive made their position clear that:

> Scottish Ministers are committed to celebrating St Andrew's Day, and the number of events taking place

on the day is growing. You may be aware last year the Scottish Executive organised the One Scotland Ceilidh in Edinburgh which was attended by 4,000 people. Scottish Ministers also attended a number of St Andrew's Day events in Edinburgh, Glasgow, Dumfries and Brussels.

The Scottish Executive wants to celebrate Scotland's achievements, its culture and history. We will continue to encourage events across Scotland on St Andrew's Day so that the people of Scotland can celebrate together. This will be the essence of the events and ideas we will take forward in future years.

Holiday entitlement is a contractual issue between employers and employees. The Scottish Parliament has no powers to create a national public holiday. The St Andrew's Day (Scotland) Bill, which was introduced to Parliament by Mr Dennis Canavan MSP, would amend Schedule 1 of the Banking and Financial Dealings Act 1971, which provides the statutory basis for UK bank holidays, by adding 30 November to the Schedule. However, the only direct effect of the Bill would be to allow for financial and other dealings to be suspended on 30 November. The Bill would allow banks to close, but they would not be compelled to do so. The Bill would have no effect on other businesses or organisations.

It would be wrong to raise expectation of a new public holiday when the Parliament cannot create one. But it should be emphasised that the Executive has no objection to employees having a holiday on St Andrew's Day. Some employers have arranged with their employees to swap an existing holiday for St Andrew's Day, and the Executive welcomes such agreements.

Mr Canavan's Bill is now under consideration by the Parliament's Enterprise and Culture Committee and the Executive will consider the outcomes of the Committee's consideration when it has been completed.[46]

The Scottish Parliament passed the St Andrew's Day Bank Holiday (Scotland) Bill on 29 November 2006.[47] Information on the Bill is available online.[48] This explains that the new St Andrew's Day

Holiday (Scotland) Bill, approved by Parliament on Wednesday, 29 November 2006, aims 'to promote St Andrew's Day on November 30 as a national celebration of Scottish identity and culture across the whole of Scotland, but the Bill in itself 'does not give any holiday rights to workers or schools in Scotland.'

The effect of the new Bill was that, 'in legal terms it allows banks in Scotland, if they wish, to close on the day specified in the Bill. In symbolic terms it signals greater celebration and awareness of St Andrew's Day and provides the option to combine that with a holiday on a specified date.'

However, the Scottish Government was not recommending that employers give a day off for 30 November. Their statement points out that, 'It is not for government to prescribe leave arrangements. We hope that employers and employees will consider together how to respond to the signal this legislation sends of greater celebration of St Andrew's Day. But the decision on whether to have a holiday is entirely up to them.' Nevertheless, the Scottish Government did decide to grant a holiday to its own staff, hoping to encourage other employers to consider following their lead by example.

As for banks, the view taken by the Scottish Government was that 'This is a matter for them.' Perhaps wisely, from Easter 1996 onwards, the Scottish Clearing Banks decided to harmonise the days on which Scottish banks closed with those in England and Wales, a decision taken 'for business reasons.'

On the question of entitlement to leave, it had to be remembered that this 'is regulated by the employment contract. Any change to this entitlement, to allow an extra day's leave on account of an additional bank holiday would be a matter for negotiation between employer and employee.

Where local authorities were concerned, they could move an existing local holiday to 30 November if they chose, but only 'after consultation with local business interests', but this would not be 'underpinned by statutory authority.' Additionally, it should be remembered that 'employers are not required by the legislation to give employees a holiday on the St Andrew's Day bank holiday. Even if they did so, they could remove another day's leave in lieu, as the Scottish Parliament did for its own staff.'

The St Andrew's Day Bank Holiday (Scotland) Act 2007 leaves flexibility for public bodies to either designate an additional holiday or use St Andrew's Day as a substitute for another holiday in the calendar.

There was also a broad consensus of popular support for the Scottish Government-led activity around St Andrew's Day in 2007. A survey of those attending the event revealed that 95% of Scottish residents thought St Andrew's Day was a good opportunity to celebrate Scotland's national identity; 71% of Scottish residents said they had not celebrated St Andrew's Day in 2006; 83% of Scottish residents said they were either very likely or likely to celebrate St Andrew's Day in 2008; 83% of Scottish residents said they were either very likely or likely to celebrate St Andrew's Day in 2008 if it was a statutory public holiday.

One area of celebration of St Andrew's Day that is regularly overlooked is the contribution made by the Church communities in Scotland. The Clutha helicopter disaster in Glasgow during the night of 29 November 2013 gave an immediacy to church services originally planned for the following day which offered a national framework for unity in prayer in tragic circumstances.

Commercial Aspects
On 30 November 1994, teasing out the commercial implications of such making St Andrew's Day a public holiday, Radio Scot-FM presenter Chris Mann looked at the arguments for and against in company with a number of interested parties.
Graham Birse, at that time public relations director of the Scottish Tourist Board (now VisitScotland), began by arguing that:

> St Andrew really helped shape the nation of Scotland. We are told that in AD 735 there was a battle at Athelstaneford in East Lothian and afterwards St Andrew was declared to be the patron saint of Alba – what is now Scotland.
>
> So, in a sense, he is our patron saint and St Andrews in Fife, of course is not merely associated with golf. It's associated with his name. It's something of a paradox that we celebrate St Andrew in our saltire cross and that throughout the world there are St Andrew societies from Hong Kong to San Francisco who, on 30 November, hold great celebrations in his name – it's become a celebration of their Scottishness because they're so far from home – yet, there isn't a holiday here in Scotland and we don't make a great fuss about it. The Scottish Tourist Board would like to see a public holi-

day, although I would stress that I don't think that those of us who work in Tourism should take a holiday on that particular day – we should be taking advantage of it.

From overseas, there's this great interest in Scottish images and Scottish culture. The other day, at the consul-general's residence in Milan, the Scottish Tourist Board held a St Andrew's Night dinner for journalists and for travel trade representatives and we had traditional Scottish entertainment. We tried to do it in a quality way – it wasn't a 'teuchter' night, but there was great appetite and interest in all the imagery associated with it. Our tourist industry is, after all, our largest now. It's worth £2 billion and 185,000 jobs depend on it. We really ought to be doing as much as we can to present our image to the world and encourage that trade.

Here in Scotland, perhaps we could do more in an educational sense about St Andrew. We could, perhaps, do more interpretation about the places his remains visited. St Andrews is an obvious place for an interpretation centre, for example. I know that the saltire flies proudly at Athelstaneford in East Lothian. Perhaps another interpretation could be introduced; more events, more pageantry, more celebration.

I think it's certainly true to say that there is a case for more economic development associated with a public holiday – that's associated with tourism. If we declared a public holiday on St Andrew's Day then I think a great deal of benefit could accrue to the tourist business, not just at a local, but at a national level. I am prepared to accept that it could provide a disruption elsewhere and I think the best solution would be to supplant one of the other public holidays, (many of which are meaningless, as far as our national heritage goes), with St Andrew's Day. It would be very useful to have a day's holiday at this time of year, because St Andrew's Day, from the tourist point of view, happily falls outside the main tourist season. We're seeking to push the season and extend it. It would also be useful for Scots to have a nice early holiday before Christmas to get the shopping done.

Ian Brown, (then working for The Edinburgh Chamber of Commerce) was equally supportive, saying that:

> I've no doubt at all that the greater use of the Saltire in trying to sell Scottish business would be highly beneficial. Before I came to the Chamber of Commerce, I spent eight years travelling Europe and the world, promoting Scottish food products. I've got no doubt whatsoever that the Scottish image is very, very strong abroad and anything we can do to strengthen that would only be beneficial. I think that there's a considerable recognition that the Saltire represents Scotland. The more that's done to use it and promote it, the better.

This brought the rejoinder from Graham Birse that:

> In fact, tartan is more likely to be recognised overseas than the Saltire. We're involved, along with other commercial partners, in a project called 'Scotland the Brand' which is about presenting Scotland and Scottish products associated with the environment and the heritage and the quality of knitwear, textiles, whisky, tourism, beef, lamb. That essentially was our message in Milan, but presented, (wrapped around, if you like), in a Scottish Heritage package which is extremely attractive and desirable.
>
> We need to do more of that in order to develop a recognition and in order to introduce the Saltire more frequently to our overseas customers. This does not have to be a nationalistic feeling – in terms of Scottish independence or separation; it communicates that we have sets of products and services that are unique to Scotland and have a premium, a quality associated with them that we're seeking to sell.

Mr Birse added that:

> I do think that, in association with St Andrew, there is an opportunity overseas to develop links; to use – or perhaps, to work alongside the St Andrew's societies and the exiled Scots, most of whom (in fact, all of whom, in

my experience) are fiercely patriotic, want to contribute something back to the Old Country. Those people, I think, would be very prepared to act as our envoys in the absence of a traditional network.

Rounding off the discussion, Ian Brown concluded that:

> There's no doubt about it that a Scottish network exists abroad and could be used. We really ought to capitalise on the ex-pat Scots living abroad to do the very best for us – to promote the country and its products. I think there is another point as well. There's a limit to how far we really ought to take the 'haggis and tartan' image. Ok, it has a limited appeal, but I think that in promoting Scotland anywhere these days, one has got to concentrate on the quality image which is very rightly deserved. It's a quality experience coming to Scotland. And that is the message we've got to put over.

How effective the saltire cross would be as a marketing tool is not entirely clear. National brands denoting country of origin are becoming increasingly important as worldwide trade barriers come down. At present, a confused message is being sent out, with the food and drink industry, the tourist trade and manufacturing firms all using variations on a number of Scottish themes. It is widely recognised that there is a need to translate the loose concept of 'Scottishness' into a strong coherent identity.

From their Strategic Development Report issued in May 1994, it emerged that the Scottish Tourist Board was seeking to market Scotland as a holiday destination to holiday-makers in England. In order to assist the development of appropriate marketing and advertising activity, the board sampled responses from people from a cross-section of society in London, Manchester, Leeds and Birmingham. Many of the respondents felt that, for attracting tourists to Scotland, a logo should include tartan. Most liked the piper because they saw him as a symbol of culture and as uniquely Scottish. The thistle was also regarded as being obviously Scottish because it was natural and colourful.

However, not all the symbols thought to be suitable for Scotland were appropriate as holiday logos. These included whisky, the stag, the lion rampant and the St Andrew's Cross. Other symbols, although regarded as potentially attractive, were not linked closely enough with Scotland: among these were the grouse, the eagle, mountains and Highland cattle.

Another key player was Scottish International. Founded in 1995, it had its aim to establish an alliance of the most successful Scots throughout the world, harnessing their knowledge, experience and influence for the benefit of Scotland. The organisation is not tied to any political, religious or other organisation and is non-profit making. The members of Scottish International were convinced of two things – first, that most of us in Scotland could learn from visitors to Scotland by asking the question, 'How do we grow international companies from a Scottish base?' Second, it was clear that Scots businessmen and women who had built and managed international companies in the USA, Hong Kong and elsewhere had for long been looking for a way of helping their country of origin and of showing an active intereste in Scottish business affairs.

As Scottish International's prospectus comments: 'If you have a drop of Scottish blood in your veins, you have reason to be proud. The success of entrepreneurs, explorers and adventurers of Scottish descent is engraved on the history of the world'. Participating in the inaugural meeting of Scottish International in 1995 under the chairmanship of the Earl of Airlie (among many others), were Sir Denys Henderson, Jackie Stewart OBE and Sir Adrian Swire.

Cash and Culture

Of all the national saints' days in Great Britain and Ireland St Patrick's is celebrated the most widely, yet it is a public holiday only in one other country – the Island of Montserrat in the Caribbean.

While the first St Patrick's Day parade in the world was held by Irish soldiers serving in the British Army who paraded through New York in 1792, the biggest St Patrick's Day parade came in 2003 with some 150,000 marchers in the Big Apple and a crowd of 15 million.

From 1968 political impetus was added to St Patrick's Day with the beginning of the 'troubles' in Ireland; this gave many Irishmen a new motivation to celebrate their roots. However, after 1995, the Irish government embarked upon a national campaign to use St Patrick's Day as a vehicle for tourism, to attract people from all over the world to Ireland and promote Irish goods and Irish companies.

Scotland began to attempt to match this phenomenally successful venture with Tartan Day (6 April), a day designated by the US Senate for recognition of the contribution made by generations of Scots-Americans to the foundation and prosperity of modern America. In

2002 a world record-breaking 'Tunes of Glory Parade' saw 10,000 pipers and drummers march through the streets of New York with thousands of Americans celebrating their historic links with Scotland. However, in 2006 voices were raised in the Scottish press as to the continued viability of the event.

But, amid the commercial drive and glitter and the public euphoria, there was a danger for Scotland's efforts to promote itself abroad. In their *The Wearing of the Green* Mike Cronin and Daryl Adair warn that, 'For the most part, St Patrick's Day is no longer a time for remembering the life of a saint and his religious message or the fortunes of the Irish nation and its people. The modern St Patrick's Day appears trite, tacky and tasteless.'[49]

If St Andrew's Day is to be a public holiday in Scotland, we must take care that the accumulated heritage represented by St Andrew the Apostle is not distorted or manipulated solely in the short-term interests of inward investment or tourism. St Andrew and all he represents is Scotland's birthright which needs to be nurtured and cherished. Scotland must not sell off the family silver – the saltire in the heart of the sun.

Religious Significance Today

St Andrew and his Saltire Cross provide a window of opportunity in culture, politics and especially religion and social action. Based in Edinburgh, St Andrew Aid Relief was formed as a charitable trust in July 1994. It was committed to raising finance and collecting and transporting humanitarian aid. From the beginning the priority was Russia. 'We chose St Andrew as our patron saint', explained co-ordinator Bob McNab, 'since he is the patron saint both of Scotland and Russia – a point well appreciated by the Russians. When we visit the four schools now on our regular calling list, we find the Saltire prominently displayed'.

Back in Scotland the Fellowship of St Andrew is a group devoted to improving relations between Christians in the West and Orthodox Christians. The former Convener of Action of Churches Together in Scotland (ACTS), the Revd Maxwell Craig, saw ecumenical possibilities in having St Andrew as a common symbol, observing that:

> Because Scotland is a nation – and one which has looked, for years, to Andrew as a focus of much that is best in our people, there is genuine significance in

observing his day each year and giving thanks for his life.

If you were to ask whether Andrew means more than, say, Ninian or Columba to most Scottish Christians, I would find myself on shakier ground. Andrew, as one of the first disciples, has a place in every Christian's calendar. But his link with Scotland is remote – perhaps more so than his links with Greece or with Russia, which also owe him special respect.

I am not one of those who believe that those we call 'saints' can intercede for present-day Scots more effectively than any others in the communion of saints. I am sure there are Christian people who do rely on the intercession of the saints for them, Andrew may be especially encouraging. As a good Presbyterian, however, my own conviction is that we have one intercessor in Jesus Christ, risen and ascended. I see no need for any other.

Having said that, I look to a time when the Church in Scotland will become united. When that happens, a patron saint may have a more central role to play – and Andrew is the one to fill that role.

The Revd Professor Robin Barbour took a more sceptical view, saying that:

It seems to me that now the actual figure of Andrew really has no significance for Scotland, and even the saltire and the diagonal cross, on which he is supposed to have been crucified, have virtually been evacuated of their original meaning. The thistle and 'wha daur meddle wi me?' probably mean more to most Scots than the death of their patron saint, following the way of his Master, yet unwilling to be thought too like him. But I suppose that if Andrew has a potential significance for the Scots that's where it lies.

Every now and then one hears references to Andrew as the one who brings others to Christ and Andrew as a fisherman; and I suppose that there's also a connexion in some people's minds with the importance of Andrew in the Greek Orthodox tradition. But I must say, I am a wee bit sceptical about his potential significance for us today.

Thinking about Scotland's patron saint brings the Revd Andrew R Morton (at the time assistant director of the Centre for Theology and Public Issues) through a journey of self-discovery:

> I confess to accepting without much thought the fact that St Andrew is the Patron saint of Scotland, even though I bear his name.
>
> However, I am glad that he is our Patron saint, as he has traditionally and properly been regarded as the prototype of the missionary – his first action was to bring his brother Simon to Jesus. So he is the Patron saint of World Mission.
>
> The more I think about this, the more important I find it. Why? Because Scotland and its Church has an honourable record of taking the gospel to the ends of the earth; this was true of the Columban Church, of the Scottish Churches in the nineteenth and early twentieth century and at other times.
>
> Sadly, the Church of Scotland at present is in grave danger of losing this worldwide and missionary vision and of retreating into a narrower and more self-preserving mood. We need Andrew to keep leading us out. So, yes, he is significant and should become more so.

Speaking in August 1994, Bishop Michael Hare Duke, former Episcopal Bishop of St Andrews, expressed his reservations about the cult of St Andrew, adding that:

> I'm happy with the Celtic saints, their legends and their fun and games. Andrew, I feel, was a strange kind of political move. It is very difficult to take those bones from Hexham very seriously, I think. It was about getting Scotland one of the Apostles. If one wanted to have any exploration into what the name of the game was with patronage and saints in the politics of the Middle Ages – that's one thing. But an actual devotional thing, I can't feel. I can see that someone like Moloch or Fergus or Blane who thumped about the hills and had something to do with Scotland – that I can see. But to actually have imported Andrew was a bit like James of

Compostella who was really all about keeping a line against the Moors.

The Most Revd Richard F Holloway, then Bishop of Edinburgh and Primus of the Scottish Episcopal Church, pointed out that:

> I am very fond of St Andrew as a character in the New Testament, especially as delineated in the three episodes in St John's gospel where he appears. He strikes me as a modest kind of man who brought people to Jesus and didn't try to push himself to the front, unlike his big brother Peter. His significance for Scotland is because he became our Patron saint in the way of these things but it would take a very ingenious intelligence to establish a particular connection between him and Scotland other than through our meditations on the New Testament.

Archbishop Leo Cushley, Roman Catholic Archbishop of St Andrews and Edinburgh commented that:

> St Andrew is the pole star for the new evangelization of Scotland. His first encounter with Jesus on the banks of the River Jordan is recorded in the Gospel of St John: 'Rabbi, where are you staying?' asks Andrew. 'Come and see,' replies the Lord. From that moment onwards, the young Andrew is completely dedicated to Jesus Christ. 'We have found the Messiah,' he exclaims with great excitement to his brother St Peter. Andrew's passion for proclaiming the good news of Jesus Christ would later see him travel to Greece. There he would have used the common language of philosophy to dialogue with the Hellenistic world. It was also there he met with martyrdom. These are the hallmarks of the new evangelization: a relationship of love with the person of Jesus Christ followed by an ability to communicate that faith in an intelligent way that is reasonable to our contemporary Scotland. St Andrew, pray for us.

The Revd John L Bell, minister, musician and Liturgical Resource worker for the Iona Community offers a corrective, saying that:

Ever since I heard the late William Barclay refer, during a St Andrew's Day sermon, to 'A dubious rickle of bones which might be buried somewhere on the East Coast', I have suspected the value of St Andrew as the Patron saint.

Apart from the fact that he had no historically verifiable connection with Scotland, he was the least important of the inner sanctum of Christ's disciples.

It is highly anomalous that a country whose religious culture owes a great deal to Calvin should have a Patron saint. It is part of the genius of Protestantism that we don't believe in saints – we just name our churches after them.

If it were worth the trouble, and if the Churches would wear it, I'd back either Patrick or Columba as the real Patron saint. Patrick would probably be the first to fall, as his Irish association clouds his Scottish pedigree – that is, if he was born on the Clyde and not in Wales.

Columba would be my front-runner for a number of reasons. Firstly, like the best saints, his fallibility and eccentricities are writ large (he came to Scotland after a copyright dispute!). Secondly, he is the prime Apostle of the Celtic Church, exhibiting more of its flair and rich spirituality than either Ninian or Patrick. Thirdly, he evangelised Scotland and (lest our Southern neighbours forget), was largely responsible for the evangelisation of North and Eastern England. Fourthly, the location of his centre of mission and his burial place can be precisely located – something which cannot be said for Andrew.

From St Andrew's Scots Memorial Church in Jerusalem, the late Revd Colin Morton offered a concluding view of St Andrew from the Holy Land:

If you stand at the Jaffa Gate or on Mount Zion and look over the Hinnom Valley, you see the saltire flying proudly over St Andrew's Scots Memorial Church. Indeed, there are many spots in Jerusalem where St Andrew's with its flag forms part of the viewer's skyline.

Before I came to Jerusalem, I had never been

responsible for flying a flag. I discovered that it was a responsibility to be taken seriously. In its very exposed position, and with desert dust, winter rain and a compass of winds, a flag does not last long. A new one soon became tattered and drab like an old regimental colour laid up in a parish church. We have to be prepared to take down the old and run up a new every six months and we are indebted to the Society of the Friends of St Andrew's whose generosity enables us to keep a supply in hand. Nevertheless, our supply has sometimes failed and there have been occasions when the white diagonals on blue could only be guessed at and even times when we have no flag at all.

Now Jerusalem is a place where it is hard to escape criticism from one quarter or another, and contrary opinions are rarely muted. But I have never experienced such fierce criticism from such a variety of sources as when we have failed to fly a decent St Andrew's flag. It has come from Scots, of course; from returning visitors and guests to St Andrew's, whatever their country, who do not like to see old traditions put at risk; from other Christians in Jerusalem who fear withdrawal of any Christian witness or presence in the Holy City; and from Jerusalemites of other faiths for whom St Andrew's, its architecture, its warmth and welcome, all that it stands for, is something precious, whose loss or diminishment would leave the city poorer and sadder.

However St Andrew came to be the patron saint of Scotland, the fact that he is means a lot here in the Holy Land. The saltire proclaims that we are Scottish; its flying here helps keep our connection to Scotland strong, and is a joy for Scots and all who love Scotland. It is a Christian cross and proclaims our Christianity, raising fewer of the bad memories among Jews or Moslems than those aroused by some other Christian symbols. And it tells of a connection that is more important still.

Scotland is one of the few countries which have as their saint one of the disciples, and Andrew was the very first to answer Jesus' call. I do not think it is wrong to say that the Scottish Christian tradition has always looked for direct, first-hand discipleship. Scots did not see their faith filtered through other traditions or authorities, political, cultural or ecclesiastical. From early days they wished to see their own church, not under another national church. The Scottish Reformation is marked by the struggle to ensure that the Kirk is responsible directly to Christ, its only head. Its worship sought to let nothing come between the worshipper and the Word of God. Apart from its dedication to the first of Christ's disciples, St Andrew's in Jerusalem has a well-known plaque within it commemorating the wish of King Robert the Bruce that his heart should be buried in Jerusalem The chord this strikes in so many hearts is a real one. There should be a direct connection between Scotland and the first source of its faith.

The Cross of St Andrew flies not only in Jerusalem, but at the Sea of Galilee Centre in Tiberias, where another Scottish St Andrew's Church stands beside the Sea. It also flies at Tabeetha School in Jaffa. We remember St Andrew in Galilee as the fisherman and disciple who went without a backward look to follow his Lord. We remember him in Jerusalem as a witness of the Resurrection, the Apostle of the new-found Church, and we can remember him in Jaffa, where he may well have set sail to carry the gospel to Greece, as the martyr who gave his life for the Master he never ceased to follow. Indeed, St Andrew makes for us a strong connection with Greece, whose patron saint he also is. The mother church in Jerusalem is the Greek Orthodox Church, tracing its unbroken descent from the Church of Pentecost. That we honour St Andrew highly, enables us better to be and be accepted as being of the one holy, universal and apostolic Church, represented with all its divisions, but more importantly in its unity, here in Jerusalem.

Scotland will never be the greatest or most prominent nation. In the Holy Land the Scottish Church is a tiny presence. I hope we can always be true followers of the man who was born in Bethlehem, taught and healed in Galilee, died and rose again in Jerusalem, whose gospel was brought to every corner of the world. I hope that we can be a blessing and support to others as Andrew was, and play our part in the feeding of the hungry and the life of the world.

St Andrew is very close and important to us in Jerusalem, no dim, distant figure. We do thank God for him and hope that Scots everywhere may always do so.

Footnotes

1   See: http://www.bbc.com/news/blogs-magazine-monitor-
    27587230 (accessed 27 May 2014).
2   Meaning 'Rock' in Aramaic.
3   PJ Casey, 'Constantius I (250?-306)', *Oxford Dictionary of
    National Biography*, Oxford University Press, 2004; online
    edition, May 2006 [http://www.oxforddnb.com/view/arti
    cle/48284, (accessed 26 Feb 2014).
4   These events are dramatised in The History Channel's DVD
    Rome: Rise and Fall of An Empire, Disc 3 'Constantine the
    Great' (Gardner Films Inc., 2008).
5   Curle, James, 'An Inventory of Objects of Roman and
    Provincial Roman Origin found on Sites in Scotland not def-
    initely associated with Roman Constructions' *Proceedings of
    the Society of Antiquaries of Scotland*, vol 66, (1931-32), p 281.
6   See: 'Rare Roman altar stones uncovered in Musselburgh'
    http://www.bbc.co.uk/news/uk-scotland-edinburgh-east-fife-
    12771243 http://www.bbc.co.uk/news/uk-scotland-edin
    burgh-east-fife-12771243.
7   For the most recent discussion of this complex event, see:
    Timothy Barnes, *Constantine* (Chichester: Wiley-Blackwell,
    2011), pp 74-80.
8   See: BBC 1 docu-drama series Ancient *Rome: The Rise and
    Fall of an Empire* (2006), episode 5, which shows the Vision
    of Constantine as a giant fiery meteorite plunging into the
    ground, followed by a black smoke-filled cross in the sky.
    Particularly good for the scenes showing Constantine paint-
    ing a white Chi Rho on his men's shields.
9   Br John Hugh Parker, email to author, 14 Oct 2012.
10 Br John Hugh Parker, email to author, 14 Oct 2012
11 Meinardus, O: 'A Study of the Relics of Saints in the Greek
    Church', *Oriens Christianus* 54, (1970), pp130-278, at pp130-
    3 quoted in Martina Bagnoli, Holger A Klein, C Griffith
    Mann, and James Robinson (eds.), *Treasures of Heaven*

(London, British Museum Press, 2011), p13.

12   The Angles were originally a Germanic tribe from the Angeln district of Schleswig who, together with the Saxons and Jutes, had invaded and conquered most of England during the fifth century AD.

13   See Davies, JR, (2010), *The Cult of Saint Constantine*. Society of Friends of Govan Old, Glasgow.

14   Cod. Guelf. 1108 Helmst, Herzog August Bibliothek, Wolfenbüttel, Germany. The text is at folio 28v-30v and also at folio 32v-35v and can be viewed online at: http://diglib.hab.de/?db=mss&list=ms&id=1108-helmst

15   Between 1440-7 Bower compiled what came to be known as the *Scotichronicon*, continuing the story of Scotland to the death of James I in 1437. Of Bower's 16 books, the first five and more are mainly the work of Fordun.

16   Walter Bower was born in Haddington and entered the community at the cathedral priory of St Andrews in his early teens. He records the foundation of the University of St Andrews in 1410 and it is assumed that his degree, Bachelor of Decrees, was from the new foundation. Bower was appointed abbot of Inchcolm Abbey (on the island of the same name in the Firth of Forth) in 1417 and remained there for over 30 years. It was on the island that he wrote his *Scotichronicon*.

17   The crossing at Queensferry was only established in the reign of Queen Margaret (c.1046-93).

18   The Royal Commission on the Ancient and Historical Monuments of Scotland (RCAHMS) places the traditional location of the Battle in East Lothian as: Canmore ID 56287 (Site Number NT57NW16).

19   *Book of Judges*, 14:14.

20   Codex Helmstedt 411 (Wolfenbüttel). See: James Houston Baxter, *Copiale* [book of copies] *Prioratus Sanctandree* (London: Oxford University Press, 1930) No 65. In Latin, the text is: 'Litera procuatoria, ad fabricam eccelsie cathedralis Sanctandree edita a Jacobo de Haldenstoun, priore Sanctandree, in theologia magistro ... brachium dextrum beati Andree apostoli ab humero usque ad cubitum, et tres digiti manus eius dextre, et patella de genu euius dextro, cum uno dente et alio osse de capite eius ... ' (folio 38 verso).

21   See: http://canmore.rcahms.gov.uk/en/site/34307/details/

st+andrews+cathedral+museum/ (accessed 28 May 2014).

22 Hall, Ursula, *The Cross of St Andrew* (Edinburgh: Birlinn Ltd., 2006), p 52

23 In 1477, the Burgundians came under the rule of the King of France.

24 See: http://canmore.rcahms.gov.uk/en/sitc/56676/ details/whitekirk+tithe+barn+and+pilgrims+houses/ (accessed 29 May 2014).

25 jelly

26 from *hypocras* – mulled wine

27 See: McRoberts, David, 'The four heid pilgrimages of Scotland', *Innes Review*, vol 19 (1968), p76.

28 *The Scotsman*, 4 May 1991.

29 See: David McRoberts and Stephen M Holmes, *Lost Interiors: The Furnishings of Scottish Churches in the Later Middle Ages* (Edinburgh: Aquhorties Press, 2012).

30 See http://www.nas.gov.uk/about/090401.asp

31 NLS Ms 3475.

32 NLS Accession number 10217/23.

33 *The Herald*, 18 Feb 2003. http://www.heraldscotland.com/ port/spl/aberdeen/it-s-official-pantone-300-is-saltire-blue-msps-rule-on-colour-of-st-andrew-s-flag-background-1.126006. See also link to the Scottish Government Flag flying Guidance. http://www.scotland.gov.uk/Topics/People/royal-ceremonial/Flag-Flying-Guidance-2012 although the link mentions 2012, it is for 2014.

34 For more information on the Honours of Scotland, see: Mgr Charles Burns, *The Scottish Sword of State* (Edinburgh: The Aquhorties Press, 2007).

35 Nona Rees, *St David of Dewisland* (Llandysul: Gomer Press, 1997).

36 Samantha Riches, *St George, Hero, Martyr and Myth* (Stroud: Sutton Publishing, 2005).

37 Thomas O'Loughlin, *Discovering St Patrick* (London: Darton, Longman & Todd, 2005).

38 Robert Pope (ed.), 'Introduction' in *Religion and National Identity, Wales and Scotland, c.1700-2000* (Cardiff: University of Wales Press, 2001), p1.

39 E Wyn James, 'The New Birth of a People: Welsh Language and Identity and the Welsh Methodists, c.1740-1820' in Robert Pope (ed.), *Religion and National Identity, Wales and*

Scotland, c.1700-2000 (Cardiff: University of Wales Press, 2001), pp15, 17.

40   See: http://www.theguardian.com/uk/2005/nov/28/ britishidentity (accessed 14 July 2014)

41   Archbishop James Ussher, *Britannicarum Ecclesiarum* (1639), cap XV (Collected Works, vi, 187-90), p 188. William F Skene, *Chronicles of the Picts, Chronicles of the Scots* (Edinburgh: HM Register House, 1867), 138-140. (*Legend of St Andrew, MCLXV* [1415], Ms. Colb. Bib. Imp. Paris, 4126). Skene notes (p li) that this 'Legend of St Andrew ... was first printed by Pinkerton in his appendix to his introduction of the History of Scotland, and is here reprinted from the Colbertine MS' in Marjorie Ogilvie Anderson, 'St Andrews before Alexander I' in *The Scottish Tradition* (Edinburgh: Scottish Academic Press, 1974), p 10, Anderson adds that Archbishop Ussher (p 187) states that it was written by a St Andrews culdee.

42   NLS Acc 10967 Address to West Lothian Covenant Association, St Andrew's Day, 1951.

43   The Ozarks Plateau is an upland region in the southern central United States covering around 50,000 square miles.

44   *The Murchison Advertiser*, 7 Sept 1906.

45   Rushworth Museum: large framed photo of the First Scottish Union Conference, September 1906.

46   Scottish Executive to author, 13 April 2006.

47   Scottish Government Protocol and Honours Team to author, 31 December 2013.

48   See: http://www.scotland.gov.uk/Topics/People/standrews daybill/questionsanswers

49   Cronin, M and Adair, D, *The Wearing of the Green* (London: Routledge, 2002), p227.

Appendix

Scottish Government support for St Andrew's Day

http://www.scotland.org/celebrate-scotland/st-andrews-day

The Scottish Government worked with 137 private sector venues to offer free / discounted entry to 196 attractions across every region in Scotland.

The Scottish Government partnered with all 182 Tesco stores in Scotland to promote the St Andrew's Day Out, Night In and St Andrew's Day Fish Dish.

Scotland's Winter Festivals funded seven St Andrew's Day events to support their media engagement, in addition to providing St Andrew's Day marketing collateral and branding for the events.

St Andrew's Day, Edinburgh – between 10,000 and 12,000
The Saltire, East Lothian – 5,250 across all events.
Oban Winter Festival – 4,284 across all events
Scotland Sings (various locations) – Participants: 2000, Audiences: 4800
St Andrew's Food & Drink Festival – 7,430 across all events
Scottish Storytelling Centre, Edinburgh – 126 across all events
Glasgow Loves St Andrew's Day – Cancelled

Across Thursday 28 – Saturday 30 November, the following ministers took part in St Andrew's Day activity:

John Swinney – Scotland Sings (SWF funded event)
Paul Wheelhouse – Melrose Abbey (Historic Scotland venue)
Aileen Campbell – Lifestyle Lanark (St Andrew's Day Out venue)
Alasdair Allan – Black House (Historic Scotland venue)
Margaret Burgess – Scottish Maritime Museum (St Andrew's Day Out venue)
Joe FitzPatrick – Jute Museum (St Andrew's Day Out venue)

Internationally, the Scottish Government engaged with Scots diaspora networks to promote their St Andrew's Day events on Scotland.org. We also shared social media content and actively engaged with the celebrations which took place around the world. We liaised with events internationally and supplied branded marketing materials. Working with the British High Commission and various Caledonian societies, branding was shared with event delegates across Bangladesh, Czech Republic, India, Russia and Tanzania. We worked with key St Andrew's Societies in Chicago, Boston, Williamsburg, New York, Washington DC, Virginia Beach, Toronto, Queensland, Bermuda and Detroit to promote their activity and the reach of St Andrew's Day around the world to our Scotland.org and Facebook channels.

Bibliography

Anderson, MO. (1974), *The Scottish Tradition*, Edinburgh: Scottish
    Academic Press.
Arnold-Foster, F. (1899), *Studies in Church Dedications of England's
    Patron Saints*, London: Skeffington & Son.
Ash, M. (1980), *The Strange Death of Scottish History*, Edinburgh:
    Ramsay head Press.
Bain, J et al., ed. (1881-), *Calendar of Documents relating to Scotland
    preserved in Her Majesty's Public Record Office, London*,
    Edinburgh: HM General Register House.
Barnes, Timothy, *Constantine, Dynasty, Religion and Power in the
    Later Roman Empire* (Chicester: Wiley-Blackwell, 2011)
Baronio, C. (1618), *Annales ecclesiastici*, vol. x [anno 586], Antwerp:
    ex officina Plantiniana.
Baxter, JH. ed. (1930), *St Andrews Copiale: Copiale Prioratus
    Sanctiandrew*, Oxford: OUP.
Bliss, WH. ed. (1893), *Calendar of Entries in the Papal Registers relat-
    ing to Great Britain and Ireland – Papal Letters*, vol. 1,
    London: HMSO.
Bower, W. (1987-1991), *Scotichronicon*, Aberdeen: AUP.
Bradley, SAJ, tr. (1982), *Anglo-Saxon Poetry*, Everyman.
Braunfels, W, (1973), *Lexikon der christlichen Ikonographie*, vol. 5,
    Vienna: Herder.
Burch, V, (1927), *Myth and Constantine the Great*, Oxford: OUP
Burns, C, (1976), *Calendar of Papal Letters to Scotland of Clement VII
    of Avignon 1378-1394*, Edinburgh: Scottish History Society.
Bute, J. (1889), 'The last resting place of St Andrew', *The Scottish
    Review*, Jan 1889. Paisley: Alex Gardner.
Bute, J. (1894), *Rectorial address delivered at the University of St
    Andrews*, London: A & C. Black.
Bute, J. (1895), *The Tomb of St Andrew*, London : Alexander Gardner.
Butler, J. (1995), *The Quest for Becket's Bones*, New Haven,
    Connecticut: Yale University Press.
Colgrave, B., ed. (1968), *The earliest life of Gregory the Great by an*

anonymous monk of Whitby, Lawrence: University of Kansas Press.

Cross, SH. and Sherbowitz-Wetzor, O.P. ed. and tr. (1953), *The Russian Primary Chronicle*, Cambridge, Massachusetts: The Medieval Academy of America Publications, vol. 60.

Cutts, EL. (1895), *Augustine of Canterbury*, London: Methuen & Co.

Dickson, T et al., ed. (1877-1978), *Accounts of the Lord High Treasurer of Scotland (Compota Thesauriariorum Regum Scotorum)*, Edinburgh: HM General Register House.

Dilworth, M. (1974), 'The Augustinian Chaper of St Andrews', *Innes Review*, No 25, Glasgow: Scottish Catholic Historical Association.

Dilworth, M. (1994), *Whithorn Priory in the late Middle Ages*, Whithorn: Friends of the Whithorn Trust.

Donaldson, G & McCrae, C. (1942-4), *St. Andrews Formulare 1514-46*, Edinburgh: Stair Society.

Dudden, FH. (1905), *Gregory the Great*, London: Longmans, Green & Co.

Duncan, TO. (1934), *Athelstaneford*, Athelstaneford: Andrew Elliott

Dunlop, AI. (1956), *Calendar of Scottish Supplications to Rome 1423-1428*, Edinburgh: Scottish History Society.

Dunlop, AI & Cowan, IB. eds. (1970), *Calendar of Scottish Supplications to Rome 1428-1432*, Edinburgh: Scottish History Society.

Dunlop, AI & Maclaughlan, D. eds. (1983), *Calendar of Scottish Supplications to Rome, vol. iv 1433-1447*, Glasgow: University of Glasgow Press.

Durkan, J. (1962), 'Care of the Poor: Pre-Reformation Hospitals' in McRoberts, D., Essays (see below).

Durkan, J. (1974), 'St Andrews in the John Law Chronicle' in *Innes Review*, No 25, Glasgow: Scottish Catholic Historical Association.

Dvornik, F. (1958), 'The Idea of Apostolicity in Byzantium', *Dumbarton Oaks Studies* No 48, Cambridge: Harvard University Press.

Fennell, J. (1995), *A History of the Russian Church to 1448*, London: Longman.

Gilbert, E. (1974), 'Saint Wilfrid's church at Hexham' in Kirby, ed., *Saint Wilfrid at Hexham*, Newcastle: Oriel Press.

Glasgow Museums (1993), *The St. Mungo Museum*, Glasgow: Glasgow Museums.

Godfrey, J. (1980), 1204, *The Unholy Crusade*, Oxford: OUP.

Gragg, FA & Gabel, LC. (1937-1957), 'Commentaries of Pius II,' in the *Smith College Studies in History*, Northampton, Massachusetts: Smith College.

Hall, U. (1994), *St. Andrew and Scotland*, St Andrews: St Andrews University Library.

Hannay, RK. (1934), *St. Andrew of Scotland*, Edinburgh: Moray Press

Hannay, RK. ed. and tr. (1913), *Rentale Sancti Andree*, Chamberlain and Granitor Accounts of the Archbishopric in the time of Cardinal Beatoun 1538-1546, Edinburgh: Edinburgh University Press.

Hannay, RK & Hay, D. eds. (1954), *The letters of James V*, Edinburgh: HMSO.

Haws, CH. (1972), *Scottish Parish Clergy at the Reformation 1540-74*, Edinburgh: SRS.

Hay Fleming, D. (1889), *Register of the Ministers, Elders and Deacons of the Christian Congregation of St. Andrew 1559-1600*, Edinburgh: Edinburgh University Press.

Howorth, HH. (1912), *Saint Gregory the Great*, London: John Murray.

Innes, T. (1978), *Scots Heraldry*, London: Johnston & Bacon,

Kazhdan, AP., ed. (1991), *The Oxford Dictionary of Byzantium*, vol 1, Oxford: OUP.

Kee, A. (1982), *Constantine versus Christ*, London: SCM.

Lamont-Brown, R. (1989), *The Life and Times of St. Andrews*, Edinburgh: John Donald.

Lindsay, ER & Cameron, AI. (1934) *Calendar of Scottish Supplications to Rome 1418-1422*, Edinburgh: Scottish History Society.

Lynch, M. (1991), *Scotland: A New History*, London: Century.

Macdonald, AA, Lynch, M & Cowan, IB. eds. (1994), *The Renaissance in Scotland: Studies in Literature, Religion, History and Culture Offered to John Durkan*, Leiden: EJ Brill.

MacEwen, A. (1913), *A History of the Churches in Scotland*, London: Hodder and Stoughton.

Macfarlane, LJ & McIntyre, J. eds. (1982), *Scotland and the Holy See*, Glasgow: Scottish Catholic Heritage Commission.

Masson, AJ. ed. (1897), *The Mission of St Augustine to England*, Cambridge: Cambridge University Press.

McCrone, D. (1992), *Understanding Scotland – The sociology of a stateless nation*, London: Routledge.

McCrone, D. Morris, A & Kiely, R. (1995), *Scotland – the Brand*, Edinburgh: Edinburgh University Press.

McGurk, F. ed. (1976), *Calendar of Papal Letters to Scotland of Benedict XIII of Avignon 1394-1419*, Edinburgh: Scottish History Society.

McKay, D. (1968), 'The Four Heid Pilgrimages of Scotland.' *Innes Review* xix, Glasgow: Scottish Catholic Historical Association

McMillan, W. (1916), *Scottish Symbols*, Paisley: Alexander Gardner.

McMillan, W & Stewart, J. (1925), *The Story of the Scottish Flag*, Glasgow: H. Hopkins.

McRoberts, D. (1976), 'The Glorious House of St Andrew' in *The Medieval Church of St Andrews*, Glasgow: Burns.

McRoberts, D. (1962), 'Material Destruction caused by the Scottish Reformation' in *Essays on the Scottish Reformation 1513-1625*, Glasgow: Burns.

Peterson, PM. (1958), *Andrew, Brother of Simon Peter*, Leiden: EJ Brill.

Purser, J. (1992), *Scotland's Music*, Edinburgh: Mainstream Publishing.

Pütter, J. (1994), *The Research Prints Catalogue*, St Andrews: Grafik Orzel.

Queller, DE. ed. (1971), *The Latin Conquest of Constantinople*, New York: John Wiley & Sons Inc.

Richards, J. (1980), *Consul of God*, London: Routledge & Kegan Paul

Ross, P. (1886), *Saint Andrew*, New York: The Scottish American.

Rubinstein, RO. (1967), 'Pius II's Piazza S. Pietro and St Andrew's Head', in *Essays in the History of Architecture presented to Rudolf Wittkower*, London: Phaidon Press.

Schmidt, S. (1992), *Augustin Bea*, New York: New City Press.

Skene, WF. (1860-62), 'Notice of the Early Ecclesiastical Settlements at St Andrews' in *Proceedings of the Society of Antiquaries of Scotland* vol. iv.

Society of Antiquaries of Scotland (1855-1994), *Proceedings of Society of Antiquaries of Scotland*, Edinburgh: National Museums of Scotland.

Storrar, W. (1990), *Scottish Identity – A Christian Vision*, Edinburgh, The Handsel Press.

Stuart, J & Burnett, G et al., eds. (1878-1908), *The Exchequer Rolls of Scotland (Rotuli Scaccarii Regum Scotorum)*, Edinburgh: HM General Register House.

Sumption, J (1975), *Pilgrimage – An Image of Medieval Religion*, London: Faber & Faber.

Thomas, C. (1973), *Bede, Archaeology and the Cult of Relics.* Jarrow: H. Saxby.

Turner, M. (1922), *The life and Labour of John Menzies Strain*, Aberdeen : Aberdeen University Press.

Watt, DER. (1969), *Fasti eccelsiae Scoticane Medii Aevi*, St Andrews: Scottish Record Society.

Wilson, S. (1983), *Saints and their Cults – studies in Religious Sociology, Folklore and History*, Cambridge: Cambridge University Press.

Index

Index

Index

Index

Index

Index